Jealousy
How to deal with it

For women

Francisco Bujan

www.vitalcoaching.com

Jealousy – How to deal with it – For women

Content

Intro	8
Jealousy – For women - Coaching	9
Jealousy – For women - Videos - Audios - PDF - ONLINE	10
Part 1 – Jealousy dynamics	**11**
What are the dynamics involved?	12
Controlling power	14
Jealousy escalation	17
The opposite of what you want	18
What works and what doesn't	20
Why it is a challenge	22
Why you want to do something about it before it is too late	25
What does it take to shift your attitude?	27
Why does it exist in the first place?	29
Why jealousy can generate pain	30
Why obsessive jealousy destroys your relationship	32
Solving unwanted jealousy or preventing it?	35
Two types of jealousy situations	37
First, he was jealous - Now I am the jealous one!	38
Male and female jealousy? Are they the same?	40
What works best with jealousy issues? Coaching or therapy?	41
Part 2 – 10 strategies to deal with obsessive jealousy	**43**
10 strategies to deal with obsessive jealousy	44
What to do with your obsessive jealousy?	47
Can you see the difference?	48
Understand the dynamics involved	49
Stop finding excuses	50

www.vitalcoaching.com

Jealousy – How to deal with it – For women

If you can't measure to other women, do something about it___ 51

Get validation from other men _____ 53

Get help! _____ 54

Redefine cheating _____ 55

Face your fears _____ 56

Work on it together _____ 57

Focus on trust _____ 58

Do it for yourself first _____ 59

Invest yourself in it! _____ 60

You have the power to shift it! _____ 61

Part 3 – How to shift an unwanted jealousy response _____ 64

How to retrain your unwanted emotional response_____ 65

You discover that your partner looks at porn _____ 67

He looks at another girl when you two are out together _____ 69

You are at home imagining he is with a girl somewhere _____ 70

He chats with a girl at a party _____ 71

His ex calls _____ 72

He has a business meeting with a gorgeous female client _____ 73

You need attention and he does not give it to you _____ 74

He does not answer your voice mail or text message _____ 75

You are not happy about your looks _____ 76

He goes out with his buddies and does not invite you_____ 77

The target? Get rid of 80% of unwanted jealousy response ___ 78

Part 4 – Jealousy mastery _____ 79

How to use my advice _____ 80

A positive force _____ 81

There was a misunderstanding _____ 84

Where to start? _____ 86

www.vitalcoaching.com

- 3 -

Jealousy – How to deal with it – For women

How to protect yourself _____ 87

Competition _____ 88

Shift to "battle" mode _____ 89

How do you choose your best jealousy weapon? _____ 90

Easy to shift jealousy? How come women get stacked with it?_ 95

I have always been the jealous type _____ 97

Can you ever change if you are the jealous type?_____ 101

Isn't being jealousy a bit like being emotionally immature? __ 102

I like being jealous! - Is there something wrong with me? ____ 103

My girlfriend is super jealous! - She thinks it's just normal! __ 104

Make sure he does not leave you over jealousy issues _____ 105

How to respond to jealousy triggers _____ 107

Why getting rid of unwanted jealousy is so thrilling!_____ 109

How women give away their power and try getting it back____ 111

Justified jealousy and when it's okay to express it _____ 114

MIRROR TACTICS! - Do EXACTLY what he does!_____ 117

Call me instead of unloading your insecurities on him _____ 120

How to stay cool always! No matter what he does!_____ 122

Part 5 - Right boundaries _____ 123

Build up peace! Give him space to relax! _____ 124

Defend his freedom _____ 125

How he will react to pressure and demands _____ 127

Don't use your controlling power to limit him _____ 129

Use your protective force rather than control _____ 130

His energy is precisely what attracts you to him_____ 132

Being clingy or desperate is a big turn off for men _____ 134

Are you committed or not? _____ 136

Is excessive jealousy emotional abuse? _____ 137

Is a little jealousy good in a relationship?_____ 138

www.vitalcoaching.com

Why does he try to make you jealous? _____ 139

Power dynamics in social situations_____ 140

Establish complicity with your partner_____ 143

If he talks a lot about other women _____ 145

He looks at other women when we go out _____ 146

He must respect your personal space _____ 147

Have a constructive chat on relationship boundaries _____ 149

How often can you have a serious talk with him? _____ 150

He's doing it again! - Why doesn't he listen? _____ 151

The long distance challenge _____ 152

How do you deal with jealousy in a long distance relationship? 156

Why supporting him financially makes you prone to jealousy_ 157

How datable is he? _____ 160

Part 6 - His exes, female friends and world _____ 163

Tell him that I don't like him being in touch with ex? _____ 164

He keeps pictures of his exes _____ 165

Your husband lies about an ex girlfriend _____ 166

Can you call his ex? Is this okay? _____ 168

Insecure about your partner's past experiences _____ 170

Is it okay for him to have a female friend? _____ 172

How to deal with him having female friends _____ 174

What to do when you see him chat with another woman _____ 175

Discuss your insecurities if he chats with other girls? _____ 177

He's got female friends but I have no male friends_____ 178

I react when he flirts with this girl at work _____ 179

Jealous of the women he works with_____ 181

He goes for after work drinks with his female colleagues _____ 184

He prefers chatting with his buddies _____ 187

I am not invited to the party _____ 189

www.vitalcoaching.com

Jealousy – How to deal with it – For women

He looks at porn _____ 190

His work always comes first! _____ 192

He systematically chooses for his kids _____ 193

Part 7 - Worried he will cheat? – Spying on him? _____ 194

Is there a way to make sure that he never cheats on you? __ 195

Afraid that your partner is cheating on you? _____ 197

My father cheated on my mother – Now I can't trust men! __ 198

Dare to express your full power! _____ 201

He cheated before! - I am worried he will cheat again! _____ 202

If he cheated before _____ 203

Should you check on him? _____ 205

Stop spying on him! _____ 207

Should you tell him that you have been spying on him? _____ 210

Should you confront him if you know he is lying? _____ 211

Part 8 – From insecurity to total trust _____ 213

What is insecurity? _____ 214

How to shift your level of power _____ 216

How to manifest security in your life _____ 218

Dissatisfaction and frustration _____ 219

Are you consumed by jealousy? _____ 221

Is there another way? _____ 223

When jealousy consumes you _____ 226

Why do you overreact? _____ 227

Trust and complicity! _____ 228

Ask yourself _____ 230

What is trust? _____ 231

Part 9 - Your exes and male friends _____ 232

Why am I jealous if I see my ex with his new girlfriend? _____ 233

www.vitalcoaching.com

Your ex has a new partner _____ 234

Jealous of your ex partner's new relationship _____ 235

My ex is chatting it up with other girls on Facebook! _____ 237

Can you be jealous of a secret crush?_____ 239

Jealous when your friend with benefits finds another woman? 240

Male friend spends all his time with his new partner! _____ 241

Conclusion _____ **242**

Intro

Jealousy can be the number one destructive force in a relationship.

It can kill love.

It can kill romance.

It can kill your partner's joy and inner freedom.

Jealousy is an instinctual response which aims at preserving the territory of your relationship.

The goal of this book is to give you effective strategies to deal with your jealousy.

Good luck and keep in touch

Francisco Bujan

Jealousy – For women - Coaching

Check this link:

http://vitalcoaching.com/coaching.htm

Jealousy – For women - Videos - Audios - PDF - ONLINE

Check this link:

http://vitalcoaching.com/jealousyforwomen.htm

www.vitalcoaching.com

Part 1 – Jealousy dynamics

When dealing with unwanted jealousy, the first step is to understand why jealousy happens and why it can become obsessive.

In the next few pages, you will discover exactly why the human mind "devised" the jealousy response and why it can turn into a destructive spiral for your relationship.

What are the dynamics involved?

Jealousy can be one of the most destructive forces in a relationship.

Jealousy is originally a positive desire to protect your relationship.

It is an instinctual impulsion which aims at protecting the couple and the family.

Now, when you express jealousy, you are often achieving exactly the opposite of what you want.

You are attacking your partner's life and freedom.

Too often, this will achieve the exact opposite of what you want.

You express control and possessiveness and destroy the harmony of what you share with him.

Is this good?

Is this an expression of love?

If your jealousy is "justified" and there is a real threat on your relationship, then it is okay.

Jealousy is a weapon and you want to master that weapon.

It is a defence mechanism aimed at protecting what you share with your partner.

Now, imagine having a sword in your hands.

This is what jealousy is.

It is a psychic weapon you can use against what threats the stability of your couple.

This "jealousy sword" can turn against what you care for the most.

It can destroy the harmony of your relationship.

This means one thing: you want to master the skills and use jealousy in a wise way.

www.vitalcoaching.com

If jealousy is simply an emotional obsessive reaction you don't control, you are most likely to hurt those around you without a reason.

You don't want that, do you?

In the next few pages, we will analyze the dynamics of jealousy and the ways to tackle the unwanted obsessive aspect of it.

When you are obsessively jealous, it is not only your partner which gets hurt, it is you and the relationship as well.

In fact, it is a loss for everyone and everything involved.

It is purely destructive.

What you want is to master your reaction.

You want to use your sword wisely only when it is really needed.

The first step is to understand the dynamics involved.

Why does it exist in the first place?

The second step is to deal with obsessive jealousy and master your instinctual reaction.

www.vitalcoaching.com

Controlling power

Jealousy comes from a need to control your territory.

You consider that your partner and relationship are "your territory" and you want to be in charge of them.

Control comes from a need to secure your life and your environment.

It is purely instinctual.

Now, you can imagine that too much control can kill life.

Too much control annihilates freedom, space, love and harmony.

It creates a constricting mind set which stops movement, freedom, creativity, fun and excitement.

Control is a natural expression of power in your life.

When you are born, you are given a reserve of it.

The first use of your controlling power is on your own life.

Control gives you the ability to stay in charge of what is yours.

The keys that you have in your pocket are a symbol of this control.

They give you the power to open the door of your house and secure your personal space.

You use control to stay in charge of your existence.

You choose actions, attitudes, thoughts, emotions, belongings, beliefs, or time frame because it is your right to control them and decide about them.

All these aspects of your existence are yours.

It is your birth right to own these aspects of your life.

As long as you apply control to what is yours, there is no conflict.

www.vitalcoaching.com

It is your right and it is a wise and healthy use of your controlling power.

Now, when you step into someone else's life and tell them what to do and when to do it, you are already stepping beyond the limits of your territory.

If someone steals from you the right to self determination, your whole spirit suffers, right?

You own your life and so does anyone else.

Your partner owns his life.

It is his birth right to decide for himself what he wants and when he wants it.

Now, when you partner with someone within a marriage or a committed relationship, you transfer part of your power to the relationship.

In fact, you accept someone else's authority and input into your life.

In other terms, part of your personal power is transferred to the couple's entity.

When you partner together, you join forces.

This is what your partner did the day he chose to have a relationship with you.

Now, what exactly was the agreement?

Did he say something like:

"From now on, you have control over my life. You can tell me what to do, when to do it and what to wear. I give you the keys of my being and you are now in charge"

Of course not!

This is not what he said.

The invisible agreement is much more along the line of:

www.vitalcoaching.com

"I stay master of my life and I partner with you to create a secure and harmonious relationship. I accept to consult with you when taking decisions and making choices simply to make sure that we are on the same wave length."

In fact, he never gave you the right to control his actions, time frame, beliefs or emotions.

All these are still belonging to him. It is still his birth right to stay master of them.

This means one thing:

When you use control to limit your partner's life, actions, attitudes or beliefs, you are already abusing your right.

You can't own someone else's life!

It is his birth right to stay in charge of his existence.

This is one of the most basic human rights:

The right for self determination.

Jealousy escalation

Obsessive jealousy and control are dead end cycles.

The more you use them on your partner, the more your relationship dies.

You are killing what you were supposed to protect: the love between the two of you.

The moment you do abuse your power, you wake up in him the need to defend himself.

He starts feeling pressured in his own space and needs to retreat to find resources to fight what tries to control him.

Obsessive jealousy is destructive.

When you use it, you achieve exactly the opposite of what you want.

It is a dead end!

The moment you use obsessive jealousy against your partner, you create an emotional cycle and reaction which turns against what you love and care for the most.

You assume that control is okay when it is not.

You assume that to protect your relationship you need to limit your partner's space and freedom.

No way!

This is 100% an abuse of the original "relationship contract".

It is a deviation of the original agreement.

No one gave you the right to control someone else's life.

www.vitalcoaching.com

The opposite of what you want

Go back to the original idea of jealousy.

The reason why nature created this instinctual response is to protect the relationship and family space.

Children and family need security.

"Justified jealousy" is your way of expressing a desire to protect your relationship's space.

The goal is to protect love, harmony and freedom.

What you want is your partner to be empowered and fulfilled.

This is what your love expresses, right?

This is what you owe to each other when you join forces within a relationship.

You partner to empower each other.

You partner because you want the best for each other.

The moment you express obsessive jealousy, you work against these goals.

In fact you destroy part of your own dream.

You attack what you care for the most: your partner's joy and life satisfaction.

What is the solution?

The solution is to use your power in a different way.

Too much control kills life force.

You want to open your arms around your partner and give him space.

You want to replace the jealousy reaction by an empowering message of trust.

www.vitalcoaching.com

Imagine how this would make you feel.

Imagine what this would bring in your relationship on the long term.

Control is a relationship killer.

Most couples who split run away from a feeling of limitation.

They feel that the relationship becomes too constricting and they need space.

It doesn't need to be that way.

The first reason to stay together is not because of control. It is because of love.

Love and trust are the solution.

You want to replace the obsessive jealousy reaction by these qualities.

In the next few pages, you will discover exactly how to manifest trust and shift the dynamics of obsessive jealousy.

www.vitalcoaching.com

What works and what doesn't

When you try to shift an emotional reaction, you need a clear vision of what to do and why to do it.

The solution needs to match on many levels.

It needs to match your own individual plan, your partner's life and the plan for your relationship.

You need to tune into a model or a mind set which works better than the one you are using right now.

In fact, you want to evolve.

The good news is that there is a natural renewal power in you.

You already have the skills in you to empower your life and design a better instinctual reaction than the obsessive jealousy one.

Shifting a negative emotional reaction is about life mastery.

The door you open when you look at your life and decide to shift things around is the door of your mind.

You suddenly realize that you have the power to actually influence your emotions and your thoughts.

In fact, what happens in your mind is your territory.

This is the ultimate place where you can have an impact.

You have the power to redesign the way you react to emotional challenges in your relationship.

How do you shift your reaction?

You identify and train a new behavior and mind set.

Ideas, thoughts and emotions are mind "objects".

You can consciously design the way you stand in your relationship.

You can choose values, attitudes, beliefs and the qualities you want to manifest.

www.vitalcoaching.com

In fact, you are the designer of your life and relationship.

Now, transformation and change don't usually happen overnight!

Shifting behavior requires understanding, focus and consistency.

However, when you realize the positive effects of a new refreshing mind set, you are most likely to adopt it instantaneously.

www.vitalcoaching.com

Why it is a challenge

Simply trying to suppress a negative emotional reaction usually does not work.

What you need to do is use your energy and power in a different way.

Imagine a powerful mountain stream.

This is your power.

It is your energy.

Your emotional reactions are fed by this energy.

If you want to shift an emotional reaction, you need to adopt a new mind model.

Simply telling to this powerful mountain stream to stop is not enough.

You need to channel its energy in another way.

In other terms, you want to consciously build trust in your relationship.

You want to secure what you share with your partner and basically develop new communication skills within your relationship.

No worries, you won't kill the passion or the intensity.

The goal is not to delete the emotional power of your relationship.

It is to express it in a different way.

Suppose you see you partner building a friendship with one of his female friends.

The goal is to keep on communicating and sharing what is happening.

If he just had a phone call with her, and you feel challenged by that, you can go to him and say something like:

www.vitalcoaching.com

"You know what? I really don't like you talking to that girl. In fact, I don't want her to call here again!"

Now, what do you feel will be the effect of your words on him?

Destructive, right?

You will clash.

He will defend his right to see who he wants and when he wants to.

In fact you could end breaking up over this issue!

Is there another alternative?

Yes! There is!

Here is what you can say:

"So, how is she doing today? Still fancying you?"

Hey? What was that?

It is teasing.

You tease him with it.

You don't try to "swallow" what you feel.

You see this woman.

She is a potential threat for your relationship.

You stay cool.

You know it is with you he shares his life.

You deal with it by teasing him about it.

You can as well say something like:

"She looks like a nice girl. You seem to have a good connection. Is she fun to work with?"

Dialogue, communication, sharing... These are magic words.

www.vitalcoaching.com

The moment you develop the ability to respond to this situation in that way, you open a whole new space in your relationship.

This is the space of trust!

It is empowering for the two of you and for your relationship!

Dare to try new behaviors and attitudes in situations like these.

You know that your mind and instincts have a whole range of possible patterns and attitudes you can manifest in your life.

Play a different card.

It does not mean that you stop playing.

You simply let go of systematically taking the possessive role and replace it with trust, respect, humor, etc.

These are attitudes you can train and develop right now.

www.vitalcoaching.com

Why you want to do something about it before it is too late

With the previous example, you realize one thing: if you don't shift your behavior, this might lead to a break up.

You don't want to break up.

You love your partner.

The reason you got this book is because you know it is in your hands.

You can be respectful <u>and</u> still express your power.

You can be an empowering presence in your partner's life <u>and</u> still secure your relationship.

You want to do something about it because if you don't, you will probably loose what you care for the most.

Tensions in a relationship can't be stretched indefinitely.

At a certain moment, it breaks.

That's unless you find another alternative.

You, your partner and your relationship are worth it.

The key shifting factor is in you.

I know that the moment you decide to do something about it, it is within your range to shift attitudes and manifest a brain new level of power and trust in your relationship.

You are the designer of it!

It is in your hands!

Don't wait another minute!

<u>Make it your top priority for at least a month</u>.

Decide right now, that no matter how far you got, this is enough!

www.vitalcoaching.com

You want a new relationship equation and you want to develop a new mind set.

Obsessive jealousy is a drain for you, your partner, your relationship and anyone who witnesses it.

www.vitalcoaching.com

What does it take to shift your attitude?

It is very simple:

It takes one to three months of focus and dedication to shift things around.

If you are ready, it even goes much faster.

Put it this way:

If you have been living with a mind set for 10, 20 or 30 years, this mind set did create habits.

These habits are emotional channels, thoughts and beliefs associated with specific situations in life.

If you tend to overreact when you see your partner chatting with another woman, you trained your mind to respond in a certain way in these situations.

Over the years, this created a mind set.

When you want to shift this mind set to an empowering feeling of love and trust, you need to retrain your emotional reaction in given situations.

You will be confronted with these challenges over a few months and develop a new way of reacting to these situations.

The goal is simple:

Create a win-win for everyone involved.

This means that there are no conflicts, draining fights or attacks on anyone's personal freedom.

Yes! It takes one to three months of focus to shift a mind set around.

You see yourself coming with new ideas and inspiration for your relationship.

You can wake up a whole new level of power in yourself and use it to protect what you care for.

You simply empower the way you stand in this.

Why does it exist in the first place?

Jealousy is an instinctual emotional response.

It is a positive defense mechanism.

When you get jealous, you send a message out: "This is my territory!"

Originally, jealousy is a very positive natural response. It is meant to protect the relationship's space.

See how it works in nature: getting jealous is your way of defending the couple's space when there is a threat.

Suppose you are a woman and your partner is flirting with another girl.

When you approach them, you send a clear invisible message.

It is an emotional projection which says something like: "get off! He's mine!"

Imagine that you have three children at home, a family to protect.

Your jealous reaction is a protective move.

You want to preserve the safety of your couple and your family.

If your partner was going out with this girl, it would threaten your relationship's and children's security.

This is why nature "created" jealousy.

It is originally a positive force meant to protect your relationship.

So, what happened?

Why can it turn into such a consuming emotion?

www.vitalcoaching.com

Why jealousy can generate pain

Jealousy generates pain when it is overused or suppressed for too long.

95% of jealousy responses can be overwhelming and out of proportion.

These extreme emotional responses become what we call obsessive jealousy.

If you take it one step further, jealousy can become delusional as well.

This means that you start imagining things which don't exist.

Obsessive jealousy happens a lot even in situations where there is no real threat. The emotional reaction still wakes up though.

Why is that?

It is an irrational response.

It is an instinctual conditioning.

It is related with lack of power and security.

You feel insecure.

You wake up jealousy as a defense mechanism.

If you were not feeling insecure and threatened, jealousy would simply not wake up.

Imagine yourself in a forest at night. Suppose it is a safe park. You know that there is no one around and you know as well that there are no wild animals.

In other words, there is no real danger.

You might still feel irrational fear.

This fear is a conditioning.

There is no real risk!

www.vitalcoaching.com

It is an <u>exaggeration of your emotional response</u>.

Take animals when there is a lightning or a storm. A dog will start shaking with fear. It is a pure instinctual response. There is no real danger.

<u>It is a conditioning which is not truly needed</u> in this specific context.

Obsessive jealousy wakes up in the same way.

It is an exaggerated emotional response.

This "response" creates pain. It is alienating.

You might be the victim of someone else's jealousy: it can be your partner who is very dominant.

You can as well be the one who is jealous.

What matters is that this instinctual defense mechanism response won't be expressed in an effective way.

It other words, <u>it won't reach its target which is to preserve the relationship's space</u>.

www.vitalcoaching.com

Why obsessive jealousy destroys your relationship

It is true!

It is crazy to realize that when you get obsessively jealous, you are actually destroying the relationship rather than protecting it.

You love someone. You get over jealous. It is a massive turn off for love!

Can you see that?

Nature created jealousy to preserve relationships, not to destroy them.

What is the basic problem?

Lack of mastery of the "jealousy emotion".

"Control" in relationships is the "generalization" of jealousy.

When you get jealous, you try to express control in one way or another.

It is your way of wanting to stay on top of what is happening.

You project an aggressive force to protect your territory.

You are "sponsored" by the relationship's spirit to do so.

It is your own natural conditioning which gives you the power to use jealousy when needed.

Nature gives you the right to get jealous.

However, when you overreact, you reach exactly the opposite of what you want: you destroy the harmony in your relationship.

The impulsion is right.

What does not match is the way you express it.

www.vitalcoaching.com

Imagine you noticed a girl at a party flirting with your partner.

You are now on the way home, chatting on the side walk with your boy friend or husband.

What you need right now is to reinforce what you share with your partner.

This is your desire: you want to get closer to him and empower what you share with him.

This girl from the party is in your mind and a bit in his mind as well.

In fact you might both be totally aware of what is happening: his mind is slightly "polarized".

He might fancy her or even have some fantasies waking up in him.

You feel that.

This is an "attack" on your relationship.

It is an attack on your space.

This is why jealousy wakes up in you.

If you bring it up, you will start a fight.

You will fight and end up being miles apart from each other.

You might have experienced this a thousand times, right?

It is always the same dynamic:

You feel like you loose control.

You feel unworthy.

You want his reassurance.

He does not give it.

You respond by attacking your partner.

You end up miles apart.

www.vitalcoaching.com

<u>This is a crisis, a fight, a drama</u>.

All this happens on the side walk while you go back home.

<u>What happened?</u>

It was a nice evening, right?

Now, you are miles apart.

You might end up crying.

You could even split up by the end of the evening if it gets worse!

<u>It is crazy, right?</u>

There was a threat. The response however was out of proportion and created the opposite effect.

The question is simple: <u>Is there another way?</u>

Solving unwanted jealousy or preventing it?

Unwanted jealousy is a consuming emotional reaction.

You don't want to be in it.

When you feel emotional pain, it is the sign that something is "dysfunctional" or went one step too far.

The best way to solve these states of insecurity is not to let them happen in the first place: Prevention.

How do you prevent insecurity?

By creating a powerful emotional foundation.

Your mind is a complex system of forces and energies. Your mind is your mind. It belongs to you.

The way you prevent insecurity is by empowering your mind.

You are in charge.

You are the designer.

This is a path of mastery and inner discovery.

Take the example of your physical health:

Suppose you get sick in the winter time. You can either keep on trying to heal when sickness appears or you can shift essential aspects of your life style.

Essential lifestyle shifts will lead to general wellness.

You can act on your diet, exercise, diminish your work load or stress level.

You can take some extra multi vitamin pills.

Do you get the picture?

www.vitalcoaching.com

Hundreds of strategies can prevent you getting sick.

Mind wellness functions in the same way:

Staying active, doing some exercise, focusing on your life goals, taking action, challenging yourself are all steps which lead to greater mind wellness.

"Mind fitness" is your business. No one can do it for you. You need sources of energy. You need stimulation. You need power. You need life force.

Relying on your partner's love and attention is not enough.

This is a long term line of evolution for you. You are in charge of your life. You are the designer of your existence.

Life design is something you do consciously.

If you feel dissatisfied or low on energy, do something to increase your level of power.

Your life and your mind are very subtle ecosystems. To keep everything in balance you need a combination of very specific qualities.

If you miss some of them, you'll generate an emotional gap.

What happens in this emotional gap? Obsessive jealousy, insecurities and other types of emotional "pains".

Understand this:

Unwanted jealousy happens for a reason.

If jealousy hurts or consumes you, it is because you lack power to protect and preserve your mind space.

The best way to prevent jealousy from waking up is to build up a stronger emotional foundation.

Extra power gives you confidence and clears insecurity.

www.vitalcoaching.com

Two types of jealousy situations

You can face two general types of jealousy situations:

- The first one is when you are jealous
- The second one is when your partner, boyfriend or husband is jealous.

Now, in the jealousy situations where you are the jealous one, you have again two general types of situations:

- The healthy ones or justified ones.

These are situations in which your partner does something which effectively justifies a jealousy response on your side

- The obsessive ones or delusional ones.

In these situations, you over react or imagine things that don't exist.

There are other cases of jealousy which can affect your life and don't involve couple situations and usually have much lower negative impact:

- Jealousy from or towards your colleagues
- Jealousy within your family for instance between brothers and sisters
- Jealousy between friends or towards girls or women in general.

90% of challenging and obsessive jealousy situations are related with couple situations.

So basically, the main challenge you face is about shifting an emotional jealousy pattern in you or dealing with this negative pattern in your partner.

Now, we have reduced the problem to its real size.

www.vitalcoaching.com

First, he was jealous - Now I am the jealous one!

This is very common in jealousy situations:

First it is your partner who is jealous and possessive.

As a response, you start being possessive as well.

While it is not an attitude you expressed originally, you picked it up and started projecting this on your partner.

When he is possessive, you tend to readapt your behavior to match his needs.

You will stop going out with your friends.

You will always call him when you are late to reassure him.

You will resist engaging in any form of non couple activity simply because you know he will react negatively.

Now, after taking all these steps to please him, you feel resentment and frustration because you did give up on activities or attitudes you enjoyed before meeting him.

What frustrates you even more is the fact that he does not seem to care and realize that he is now the one going out with his mates or not calling you when he is late.

He will accuse you of being possessive and demanding, right?

What is the solution?

Freedom and relationship boundaries work both ways in your couple.

You have to rewind and go back to the original situation before you met your partner.

You want to learn to be free again.

You need to reconnect with what you used to do before meeting him.

Why?

www.vitalcoaching.com

<u>Because being in a couple does not mean you have to give up your individuality.</u>

You gave up a precious part of your being: your freedom.

You sacrificed it in the name of his needs and this is the exact moment you started feeling frustrated.

Why do you feel frustrated?

Because he does not reciprocate!

He believes that expressing his freedom is his right.

He uses that right!

Remember that relationship boundaries (how much time, space and freedom you have for yourself for instance) work both ways.

What is okay for him is okay for you as well.

Tell him this and take back what was stolen from you in the first place.

This will bring back the balance of power to the right middle place.

He might react negatively and behave possessive again.

We enter now into a new set of challenges: "How to deal with a jealous partner".

If he is open for it, ask him to check the "Jealousy – For men" area on vitalcoaching.com.

www.vitalcoaching.com

Male and female jealousy? Are they the same?

In theory, yes!

Jealousy in men and women aims at the same thing: trying to protect your relationship!

Now, the way women and men express it is actually quite different.

Guys tend to have the power to control a woman's life. When a guy gets jealous, he will tend to be emotionally abusive.

This emotional abuse dimension is a key difference.

A woman will express her jealousy more in the sense of emotional insecurity and turn this against herself.

Now, of course, you do have situations where women take an abusive position and control a man's life.

This happens especially if the woman is in a position of power and the guy tends to be soft.

In that case, emotional abuse and control will naturally happen.

You can as well have guys who are jealous but emotionally weak who turn jealousy into a self destructive pattern for themselves.

They express it as insecurity and you see them totally disempowered when they express their jealousy.

Remember that jealousy is always related with the desire to bring back a sense of security in your life.

It is related with the desire to protect the couple's unit.

When this couple unit is threatened, jealousy tends to wake up.

Now, if you are naturally very insecure in life, you will naturally wake up the jealousy pattern more often because you rely much more on your partner and couple for emotional security.

www.vitalcoaching.com

What works best with jealousy issues? Coaching or therapy?

Let's first check what each approach does, ok?

Therapy originates in the medical profession and focuses on healing.

When you go to see a therapist, you believe that you need healing and that somehow, your present emotional reactions are dysfunctional.

Coaching originates in the sports and business field. It focuses on performance, success and life satisfaction.

You go to see a coach because you want more from life! The number one quality you get from coaching is extra power.

That said, if you are a jealous guy, what do you feel you need the most? Healing or extra power.

To tell you the truth, I think it's great you have the choice!

I know what I would choose myself, but of course my opinion is biased because I am a coach! Of course, I believe 100% in what I do because I see the results.

What about hypnotherapy? Well the results we seek are again the same, but the way to get there are quite different.

With coaching, my goal is to give you extra power and make sure that after a couple of sessions or going through the book and MP3 audios, you have all the tools and skills you need.

I like you to own the transformation process. I like you to be fully awake.

You don't need to be in an hypnotic trance state for this material to impact and make changes in your life.

I did explore the possibility of integrating a couple of hypnotherapy techniques in this material or in my coaching but consciously decided not to go that way.

www.vitalcoaching.com

Why? Not sure. It simply did not match with my approach energy wise.

Somehow I felt it was side tracking the core message I wanted to give you:

You are in charge!

You are in the control seat!

You own the transformation process!

It is extra power you need not healing!

The choice is yours really!

Part 2 – 10 strategies to deal with obsessive jealousy

10 strategies to deal with obsessive jealousy

When it comes to unwanted or obsessive jealousy, the final challenge is about using your emotions is a different way.

If you know your jealousy is unjustified and you want to shift it to something more positive, you have to <u>retrain your instinctual reaction</u>.

The goal is simple: replace the jealousy emotion by an empowering feeling of trust.

The key question is:

<u>How to retrain an instinctual response?</u>

Here are some key steps you can take:

- **The first step is to understand the dynamics involved**.

  Originally, Jealousy is an instinctual response aimed at protecting a relationship. This is the first goal of your instinctual response. However, when you express obsessive jealousy, you are achieving exactly the opposite. You are destroying your relationship. <u>Excessive possessiveness is a relationship killer</u>.

- **Stop finding excuses**.

  The reason you express obsessive jealousy is because a part of you justifies it. You find superficial excuses and imaginary threats to be over possessive. <u>Don't hide yourself</u>. You know what you are doing and you know it is wrong.

- **If you can't measure to other women, do something about it**.

  Get yourself new skills, develop a new look, remove what is unattractive in you. Work on your personality and personal power.

- **Get validation from other men**

www.vitalcoaching.com

The reason you become possessive is because you feel your self worth depends on your partner's exclusive attention. The moment you get some of this from other men (male friends, light flirts, etc) you feel empowered and valued.

- **Get help!**

  Sometimes, the only thing you need is a second opinion to make you open your eyes. Have a few sessions with a coach or a therapist. Do this alone or with your partner. A close friend's opinion might do the trick as well.

- **Redefine cheating**

  Chatting with one of his female friend's is not cheating. A light flirt is not cheating. Cheating is not a fantasy, it is an action. You can't control someone's thoughts. The real limit has to do with exclusivity in sex and other aspects of intimacy. Is he crossing the line or not?

- **Face your fears**

  If you believe he is way out of line if he goes partying on Saturday night, go with him one time and check it out. You might realize that your imagination does play tricks on you. Confront your beliefs with real facts. Don't use vague feelings as a justification for possessiveness.

- **Work on it together**

  Sometimes you strengthen the jealousy pattern in each other. You get jealous and possessive. He reflects this pattern and limits your space as well. If this is the case, work on it together and tackle the negative pattern in both of you at the same time.

- **Focus on trust**

  Trust is the real alternative to jealousy. When possessiveness is gone, it is replaced by an empowering feeling of trust. Wake up this quality in your relationship and choose to trust your partner whenever you can.

- **Do it for yourself first**

  Being obsessively jealous is energy consuming for you. It is a waste of your precious time. You are the one who will first

www.vitalcoaching.com

benefit from a healthier mind set. <u>You deserve it</u>. Your partner will naturally be empowered by it.

You will realize one simple thing: the moment you do take these steps, you will already manifest new levels of mutual trust in your relationship.

It takes some time and dedication to give your emotions a new program.

<u>Consistency is the key</u>.

This shift won't happen overnight. Give yourself the target to solve 90% of this issue within 1 to 3 months.

<u>Make it your top priority</u> at least for the first month.

Use your will power, determination and whatever you need to break through.

<u>Invest yourself in it</u>.

The moment you set your mind into empowering your relationship, you invoke new refreshing forces in the core of what you share with your partner.

Take action! You and your relationship are worth it!

www.vitalcoaching.com

What to do with your obsessive jealousy?

Give yourself new fighting tools.

Jealousy is a battle strategy. Jealousy is a weapon.

You wake up this weapon when there is a fight between two energy realities:

- On one side there is you, your life and your mind
- On the other side, there is a challenging force: another woman

Obsessive jealousy happens when you get overpowered by this challenging force.

You can be jealous of a threat which does not even exist on the physical level. It can be a pure psychic energy.

You can be jealous of one of your partner's ex who is out of the picture for many years.

You can be jealous of a movie star.

The dynamics are always the same.

There is a battle between two forces: your mind and another reality.

This conflict creates a jealousy response in you.

Basically, this threat is eating up your confidence and generating insecurity.

Being jealous is your "best" response at defending yourself.

It is your best "shot" at that moment.

Again, it is 100% an irrational and instinctual response.

The reason it consumes you is because you need too much of it to overcome this threat.

www.vitalcoaching.com

You feel a threat and no matter how hard you try, your "jealousy weapon" does not seem to be enough.

You need other tools to protect your psychic space.

Why does this obsessive emotion wake up in your mind?

Because you don't have enough power to protect your mind space.

You can see your mind territory as a castle with thick walls.

When you get jealous, it is because there is a threat.

If this threat stays in the distance, it won't consume you.

If it manages to "come into your mind", it will consume you.

Can you see the difference?

Understand the dynamics involved

Originally, jealousy is an instinctual response aimed at protecting a relationship.

This is the first goal of your jealousy instinctual response.

However, when you express obsessive jealousy, you are achieving exactly the opposite.

You are destroying your relationship.

Excessive possessiveness is a relationship killer.

There is no way around this.

You must know that when you use control on your partner, you kill his joy and pleasure to be alive.

You destroy your partner's life.

At the end, he will wish you never got together and even never met.

He will run away and never come back.

You must know this and repeat it to yourself over and over again until you decide to shift your attitude.

If you don't, consider this your last warning.

I am giving it to you in his name and in the name of your relationship.

Abusing your partner's freedom is not okay!

It will never be!

Your role in his life is to protect his space and freedom; not to use your power against him.

Stop finding excuses

The reason you express obsessive jealousy is because a part of you justifies it.

You find superficial excuses and imaginary threats to be over possessive.

Don't hide yourself.

You know what you are doing and you know it is wrong.

There is a common belief amongst women, men and couples that when you are in a relationship, you have to give away your life to your partner.

This idea is old fashioned and goes 100% against the human spirit.

The human spirit is and wants to stay free!

You can express your power and be a fully dignified female without having to control a man's life to feel that way!

You can't own another person's life!

So, don't try to justify obsessive jealousy in the name of protecting your relationship.

There is no excuse for obsessive jealousy.

www.vitalcoaching.com

If you can't measure to other women, do something about it

Get yourself new skills.

Develop a new look.

Remove what is unattractive in you.

Work on your personality and personal power.

Your present limits are not your real limits.

If you feel insecure about your talents and skills, take action and develop them.

Society is competitive.

There is no doubt about it!

You want to play fair.

If you feel you miss the "competitive edge" in the love and dating scene, develop new skills.

Hoping that your partner will stay with you because you limit his space is a big mistake!

It might rather lead to the end of what you share with him.

If you want to enjoy long lasting love and an exciting partnership, make sure you pick up some of your personal challenges and keep evolving and developing yourself.

Here are the main areas in which you can get new skills:

- Business
- Career
- Self growth
- Health and body
- Social life
- Spiritual development
- Relationship skills
- Etc.

www.vitalcoaching.com

The possibilities are infinite; so play the game and play it fair.

If you believe that what you have to offer does not measure, take steps to develop what is missing.

This will give you the extra confidence kick you are looking for.

Get validation from other men

The reason you become possessive is because you feel your self worth depends on your partner's exclusive attention.

The moment you get some of this from other men (male friends, light flirts, etc) you become less desperate and feel more valued.

What your partner gives you is love and validation.

Now, the moment you realize you can get these from other sources, it empowers the way you stand in your relationship.

It is okay to have a light flirt.

It is okay to sometimes fantasize about other men.

It is okay to loosen up slightly the boundaries of your relationship and realize that there is a world out there.

Obsessive jealousy can be the result of isolation.

You isolate yourself and the relationship within a cocoon of energies.

What you want now is open up and connect.

Your partner stays number 1.

Being in a committed relationship must not stop you from interacting with the opposite sex.

Get help!

Sometimes, the only thing you need is a second opinion to make you open your eyes.

Have a few sessions with a coach or a therapist.

Do this alone or with your partner.

A close friend's opinion might do the trick as well.

There is no shame in getting some targeted help or support with that.

In fact, it is one of the most empowering steps you can take.

No need to reinvent the wheel!

Many people have been where you are right now.

Why not use their experience?

There is a world of knowledge and expertise you can tap into.

If you feel challenging to train a new behavior by yourself, be wise and connect with fresh sources of support and inspiration.

No need to take the role of a victim or therapy patient.

This is not what it is.

You are healthy and perfectly functional.

Now, what you want is simply to gain extra power and new skills.

You want to discover new ways of handling a given challenge in life.

Look around you.

Be discriminative and do connect with sources of empowering support which can help you take your life to the next level.

www.vitalcoaching.com

Redefine cheating

Chatting with one of his female friends is not cheating.

A light flirt is not cheating.

Cheating is not a fantasy, it is an action.

You can't control someone else's thoughts.

The real limit has to do with exclusivity in sex and other intimacy aspects.

Is he crossing the line or not?

Cheating is a very specific action.

It involves intimacy.

Now, if you react because your husband did cheat on you, it is probably justified, right?

What are the facts?

Who does he share his life with?

Is it with you or with a woman he saw once at a party?

You did catch a glimpse of excitement in his eyes?

There is nothing wrong with that!

Your partner can receive validation from other women without this being a real threat on your relationship.

In fact it is empowering for your couple.

Put it this way: Even though he has the choice, it is still with you he decides to be.

You win! He wins!

Face your fears

If you believe he is way out of line when he goes partying on Saturday night, go with him one time and check it out.

You might realize that your imagination does play tricks on you.

Confront your beliefs with real facts.

Don't use vague feelings as a justification for possessiveness.

Real facts!

Most obsessive jealousy is based on delusion.

It comes from envisioning events, feelings and thoughts which do not exist.

It is a delusion.

Can there be a real threat?

Yes! Of course!

No need to play dumb either.

You can stay awake and aware but measure with exactitude the real extent of a threat on your relationship.

Step away from vague feelings and confront yourself with real facts.

If you have doubts, take steps and check them out.

www.vitalcoaching.com

Work on it together

Sometimes you strengthen the jealousy pattern in each other.

You get jealous and possessive.

He reflects this pattern and limits your space as well.

If this is the case, work on it together and tackle the negative pattern in both of you at the same time.

Dialogue, trust, love and partnership are qualities you invite consciously in your relationship.

These are the nectar of what you share.

They are the core values of your relationship.

The best way to solve tensions is with dialogue and diplomacy.

Your relationship is an ever evolving organism.

When you reach the limits of what you can do together, there is always a next possible step.

This often involves gaining new relationship skills.

Long term relationship success is about inviting change and renewal in your partnership.

Dare to look beyond the limits of what you already know.

It is a vast topic and there is another book available on the topic of relationship empowerment.

Check the relationship section on vitalcoaching.com for more on that.

Focus on trust

Trust is the real alternative to jealousy.

When possessiveness is gone, it is replaced by an empowering feeling of trust.

Wake up this quality in your relationship and choose to trust your partner whenever you can.

Trust means that you open space in your partner's life rather than limiting him.

You give him power, energy and validation as a human being.

Trust is one of the key foundation qualities in your relationship.

It is one you can invite and consciously develop by choosing for it whenever you can.

Trust empowers your relationship.

Tell him you trust him.

This creates a unifying bond between the two of you.

Do it for yourself first

Being obsessively jealous is energy consuming for you.

It is a waste of your precious time.

You are the one who will first benefit from a healthier mind set.

You deserve it.

Your partner will naturally be empowered by it.

The moment you decide to shift a negative pattern in you, you empower your life straight away.

In fact, it gives you an immense feeling of victory and satisfaction.

You are the first one who wins from it.

You shift your emotional base and stop wasting your time trying to control something you can't control.

All this energy which was used for fighting and worrying is now free.

You can reinvest it in various ways in your life and relationship.

This is about gaining long term life mastery.

Mastering an unwanted jealousy reaction is one of these tests you face in life.

Now, the moment you understand how this works, you open a door to new possibilities.

This is about your mind!

This is about your life and the satisfaction you gain from it!

Realize that you are the architect!

You are the designer of your existence!

Invest yourself in it!

You realize one simple thing:

The moment you do take these steps, you already manifest new levels of mutual trust in your relationship.

It takes some time and dedication to give your emotions a new "program".

Consistency is the key.

This shift won't happen overnight.

Give yourself the target to solve 90% of this issue within 1 to 3 months.

Make it your top priority at least for the first month.

Use your will power, determination and whatever you need to break through.

Invest yourself in it.

The moment you set your mind towards empowering your relationship, you invoke new refreshing forces in the core of what you share with your partner.

Take action!

You and your relationship are worth it!

You have the power to shift it!

There is a common belief that your mind is somehow out of reach and that your emotions simply happen.

This is not true.

You have direct ways of accessing and shifting what happens in your mind.

Your emotions are not a given set of patterns you can't influence.

If you tend to be over jealous and you know this can destroy your love life, you are the one who will do something about it.

You are the person who has the greatest influence over your thoughts, believes, emotions, actions and attitudes.

Part of what you do is an automatic response, right?

Now, you were not born with this instinctual response.

An instinctual response is the result of a conditioning.

You simply developed a given emotional response to situations which challenge your position in a relationship.

An emotional response is not a fixed pattern.

You can change it!

Does it happen overnight?

No!

Will it take some effort, focus and dedication?

Yes!

Is it within your reach?

100% yes!!!!!

A mind pattern is a set of emotions, beliefs and thoughts.

www.vitalcoaching.com

The "jealousy" mind set is only one possible mind set in a relationship.

The "trust" mind set for instance is another one.

Even within the jealousy mind set, you can play with the way you invest yourself in it.

This is not fixed.

You can play with humor.

You can play with "playing jealous".

Most men enjoy seeing that you are ready to fight for them and for the love you share.

A bit of jealousy game can be welcome.

Now, if your power and jealousy weapon turns against the person you love, you obviously go one step too far.

Perfect harmony and balance in a relationship is created by a perfect combination of qualities.

You want to experiment and find out for yourself what works and what doesn't.

This book is the first step of your solution.

The real solution is to take action and apply these strategies.

Read this book again.

Go to online forums.

Share ideas with other women.

Establish dialogue and diplomacy in your relationship.

What matters is that you don't stand still with it and keep evolving and learning.

This challenge is an opportunity to grow.

It is an opportunity to empower what you share with your partner.

www.vitalcoaching.com

You can come out of this closer than ever.

Accept the fact that it is a battle of forces and energies and accept as well to do what it takes to win this battle no matter what.

You are not a victim.

Your couple is not a victim.

You are simply facing one of these challenges and your goal is to win this battle.

No one needs to loose.

You can both come out of this immensely stronger and empowered!

Part 3 – How to shift an unwanted jealousy response

How to retrain your unwanted emotional response

Once you mentally understand the dynamics of unwanted jealousy, you still need to apply a set of behavior or attitude shifts so that the way you relate to yourself and your partner really changes.

Some of these techniques are quite challenging and upfront.

Don't be offended and stay open minded, okay?

The goal is to practice new behaviors.

You practice a new behavior each week for a period of 3 months until you have a whole new set of behaviors and strategies you can easily apply to replace key unwanted jealousy responses.

The goal here is not to eradicate all jealousy.

As we mentioned earlier, some justified jealousy is good to maintain the strength of your relationship.

This jealousy is okay as long as you feel you are on top of that emotion rather than enslaved by it.

So, here is how this training works:

At the beginning of each week, you choose one key attitude or situation you want to work on.

It might be the way seeing porn negatively impacts on you, your insecure attitude in social situations or the way you communicate with your partner when he does not give you the security your expect for instance.

In the next page, I describe 10 key situations which can trigger an unwanted jealousy response.

After that, we will identify the exact opposite empowering behaviors which suit you best.

The goal is to create a new set of skills and attitudes you can tap into any time.

www.vitalcoaching.com

You can work through these sets of skills systematically or your can choose the one that matches your situation and then, apply the retraining strategy which is given to you.

The goal is to have a set of new skills you can apply any time you feel challenged.

If you already practiced these skills, you'll be able to respond to the challenge much more effectively of course.

In the next few chapters, I will describe a key jealousy situation with a new attitude which can effectively tackle your jealousy response.

The strategies or solutions I share with you are of course only suggestions.

If you take the "looking at porn" example for instance, I am not saying that you should accept it, simply that if you don't like your jealousy response, there are ways to respond in a different way.

<u>For each situation, you are welcome to reinvent a solution which suits you best if you want to</u>.

You are free of course

Here are the examples I focused on in the coming chapters:

- You discover that your partner looks at porn
- He looks at another girl when you two are out
- You are at home imagining he is with a girl somewhere
- He chats with a girl at a party
- His ex calls
- He has a business meeting with a female client
- You need warmth and attention and he does not give it to you
- He does not answer your voice mail or text message
- You are not happy about your looks
- He goes out with his buddies and does not invite you

In these examples, I take the role of your inner voice and speak as if it was your inner self talk.

www.vitalcoaching.com

You discover that your partner looks at porn

Unwanted jealousy response

Why is he cheating on me? How come he has to look at other girls when he has me?

This probably means that he does not love me!

He is probably not happy with me.

All guys are real jerks. I can't believe that he is using me for sex like that.

I will confront him and tell him what I feel about his dirty behaviors.

I am going to force him to stop with this. It's either he complies or I am out of this relationship.

Why would a woman have to take that!

He should be ashamed of himself

Your new response

I realize that there is a world about him I don't understand yet.

In fact, there is nothing dirty about porn. It is just an expression of our human needs.

If we would explore our own sexual needs and fantasies together, this might give him an avenue to share that part with me.

It's just a girl on a screen. I know he would never act on it.

It's not cheating because he does not act on it.

He never cheated on me.

www.vitalcoaching.com

Loving someone means embracing everything about this person, even his darkest secrets.

I know I can't control his actions.

Their fake breasts and horny attitudes are very artificial! Why would I be threatened by that?

It's an occasion to explore a part of our relationship we did not conquer yet.

Let's have an adult discussion about what is behind all that without attacking or challenging him.

He's not a little boy and I am not his mum! We are two grown up adults who enjoy each other immensely.

I can simply ask him to close his last porn window when he's done. Nothing to be worried about.

If this is what he likes, why not get him a man's magazine. It does not need to be porn though. Some exposed female flesh will do! ☺

Let's tease him on that!

www.vitalcoaching.com

He looks at another girl when you two are out together

Unwanted jealousy response

Why does he look at her? Does he know her?

Am I not pretty enough?

Why does he not give me his attention?

Hey! Look at me! You want to date her or something? Now, I am really angry!

Your new response

Pretty girl indeed! If I was attracted to the same sex, that's the kind of girl I would be attracted to.

You like her? Why don't you go and ask her out?

Threesome mister?

Hmm... Let me see if I find an attractive guy myself...

He is just looking, not touching!

If I was a guy, I would probably do the same

It's my hand he's holding, right?

You are at home imagining he is with a girl somewhere

Unwanted jealousy response

He said he would be home by 6!

I spend my life waiting for him!

He's probably having a drink with his friends chatting with this attractive female PA he works with.

I knew this would happen! He is cheating on me right now!

Your new response

Fair enough! He's probably relaxing with his mates

Let's give him a call, something might have happened and he is delayed.

His boss always overloads him!

It's amazing how dedicated he is to his work. It is so nice to be with a guy who takes profession and money seriously. I can really rely on him!

Excellent! This gives me some space to relax and wok on these new yoga postures I just learned.

Time to call Cindy and have some girly talk!

Let's go out and have a drink with my ex. He (Paul, my ex) has been telling me he wanted to have a chat about our kids for some time already. I'll leave Jim (my husband) a note.

www.vitalcoaching.com

He chats with a girl at a party

Unwanted jealousy response

Nobody to talk to and now he is even flirting with this top model.

She's so much prettier than I am.

How come he always talks with attractive girls?

I thought we were going out together!!!

What about _my_ drink?!!!

I can see you fancy her!

Your new response

So lucky to have found him first!

Hey girl! He is mine! Don't touch!

I need some extramarital male validation! Let's find a nice attractive hank!

I love that we can be like two strangers and still feel this invisible complicity between the two of us.

Let's go and get him back!

She's a bitch anyway!

What a stupid face!

What are you hiding under these layers of make up?

His ex calls

Unwanted jealousy response

I told you I don't want your ex to call here!

Her again!

Leave us alone!

Why are you trying to steal my husband?

I bet they are still in love!

Just when we were getting ready for dinner!!! It's always the same!

Why doesn't she find a new man rather than being so clingy on mine?!!!

What now?!!!

Your new response

It's with me he decides to be!

Funny how distant he is when he speaks with her. They certainly don't share the intimacy we have.

I trust you! It's such a great feeling!

When you are done, I'll jump on you and make love with you.

The perfect moment to sneak out and check my profile on my space. See if this Latino god winked at me again…

Honey, I'm off to the gym!

www.vitalcoaching.com

He has a business meeting with a gorgeous female client

Unwanted jealousy response

They surely are attracted to each other.

Business meeting??? At 8pm???

How come I'm not invited?

Why didn't he send his colleague? He's into something for sure!

Your new response

She's married and already told me how much she loves her husband.

He is very dedicated to his work.

I love the fact that no woman can threaten what we have.

Great deal in view! This means extra bonus for us and Caribbean holidays for New Year!

This sure will pay for my year's gym membership!

I love what he said last night about what we share...

www.vitalcoaching.com

You need attention and he does not give it to you

Unwanted jealousy response

How come he's so cold to me lately?

He used to be different two years ago when we first got together

Is he having an affair? All these late nights at work?

I want you to hug me now!!!!

You never say "I love you" anymore!

I worked the whole day too!!! I am still here!!!

Your new response

Pretty challenging time for both of us. No wonder we are both stressed. Now is the time to really stick together and tell him how much I care.

Let's put on something sexier.

True, I should work out a bit more. I haven't been taking care of myself lately.

This situation at work is obviously stressing him. No wonder that they say that 50% guys are too tired to have sex when they come back from work.

Let's see if we can have a non challenging chat about this in the next few days.

He does not answer your voice mail or text message

Unwanted jealousy response

Why doesn't he answer!!!

Let's call him again!

Why is he playing games with me???

I can't believe I trusted him! There is something wrong!

How come I always come last?!!!

What's so difficult about sending me a quick Text?

Your new response

Well, he's probably busy with a client.

Right... I forgot. He already said to me that he does not want to answer personal calls or text messages when he is at work. It distracts him. Fair enough. Okay with me. He does not need to be focused on me 24 hours a day.

Well, I'll make my own plans then.

I'll decide without him. In fact it makes it simpler for me to take this decision alone.

I hate it too when he calls me at work and wants to me to say sweet things when all my colleagues are listening...

www.vitalcoaching.com

You are not happy about your looks

Unwanted jealousy response

She's much prettier than I am

I never liked the shape of my nose

How come you never tell me you like me?

I really feel insecure. I need him to call me and be with me

Your new response

Now is the time to take a serious decision and commitment!

If I train twice a week, I'll be back in shape by Christmas.

In fact he shows me every day that he likes me the way I am

Let's go shopping!

Pretty sexy this new outfit!

This $50 is for a special treat! I deserve it! Sauna? Hair? 10 lessons kickboxing class?

He goes out with his buddies and does not invite you

Unwanted jealousy response

He leaves me alone here!!!

How come he never takes <u>me</u> out?!!!!

I can't believe he does that to me!

I thought we were getting married!

I'm sure they go to strip clubs!!!

Your new response

I am okay with it but I'll ask him to tell me a couple of days before so that I don't make plans with him for that day.

Perfect timing to check this new café with Amanda!

Great! I needed a break anyway. Popcorns and TV this evening!

I'll give him a party when he comes home... Let's send him a sexy Text so that he knows something's waiting for him.

These friends of him are great, especially Mark. I would fall for him if I was not with Cliff already... I am sure that Mark fancies me by the way. I can see it in the way he looks at me.

It's good he has a team of mates with who he can relax and have some fun.

Guys need some freedom. Pretty normal to go out and have fun every now and then.

www.vitalcoaching.com

The target? Get rid of 80% of unwanted jealousy response

This is a simple target you can focus on.

The goal is to train these new positive behaviors and reach your target within one to three months.

You know that you reach your target the moment you realize that 80% of your unwanted jealousy responses are gone.

I only described 10 key situations.

Of course, you might face a jealousy challenge which is not covered here.

If it is the case, write down a phrase or sentence summarizing your challenging situation.

Under this sentence write down "Unwanted jealousy response" and "My new response" the way I did for these previous examples.

After that, take a moment to think about what your unwanted jealousy self talk is saying.

Then, write down a few sentences which summarize what positive self talk would look like.

I know that in the beginning, it can be challenging.

Once you start, you'll notice it flows easily.

If you really don't know how or where to start, sign in for a coaching session and I'll help you further with this.

After a few weeks of practicing these self talk techniques, you can radically shift the way you respond to challenges.

Make it your top priority and focus on it actively. You'll be amazed of the results you get.

Part 4 – Jealousy mastery

In this book, we focused on two types of jealousy reactions we already mentioned earlier:

- The healthy ones or justified ones.

These are situations in which your partner does something which effectively justifies a jealousy response on your side

- The obsessive ones or delusional ones.

In these situations, you over react or imagine things that don't exist.

In the next few pages we will analyze the best strategies to express your jealousy in a healthy way.

In other terms, we will look at situations where jealousy is justified.

In these situations, the natural reaction is often to want to suppress this jealousy emotion.

In fact, in these cases, jealousy is actually useful because it gives you the tools to educate your partner.

All you need is to be able to express jealousy wisely in a way which effectively empowers your couple rather than destroys it.

Justified jealousy is a weapon aimed at protecting your relationship and couple space.

The goal is not to give it away. It is to use it wisely.

See jealousy as a sword you have in your hands.

A sword can sometimes turn against what you are precisely trying to protect.

What you want is to master the skills to use it effectively.

www.vitalcoaching.com

How to use my advice

In this book, I check lots of real life situations and propose solutions for these challenges.

These are only guidelines.

These solutions are not unique.

What matters at the end is that you trust and follow your instinct.

Your situation is always unique.

However, certain emotional reactions and relationship patterns simply never work.

Some other patterns are usually effective.

You can become a master at playing with these behaviors and attitudes.

Remember that you are the architect of your relationship.

You are the one who decides what happens in it.

A positive force

What I am about to say will probably shift everything you heard before about jealousy:

Some jealousy is good!!!

It is originally a positive constructive force in your life!

You might believe that because you are jealous, there is something wrong with you.

There isn't!

Some jealousy is perfectly fine and healthy.

Jealousy comes from a positive desire to protect your relationship.

The term jealousy comes from the Latin word "zelosus" which means "full of zeal".

In other words, by etymology, jealousy and zealous are one same concept.

If you take this idea one step further, jealousy is basically a deep desire to do it well, to do it right!

Other synonyms for zealous are: enthusiastic, passionate and fervent.

Zealous involves as well the idea of being fanatical, obsessive and extreme.

This is precisely the place where jealousy can go one step too far and consume you.

If jealousy is simply a desire to get it right, why does it hurt you?

Why can jealousy burn your from the inside and create this inner turmoil?

It hurts you precisely because of this obsessive or extreme aspect associated with it.

It hurts you as well when it does not manage to find its way.

www.vitalcoaching.com

<u>Jealousy is a psychic weapon</u>.

You use it in the battle for power. It is a tool you want to master. It can burn because it is extremely powerful.

It can burn you because it can trigger an inner conflict.

Something in you believes that jealousy is wrong.

Something in you wants to suppress it or delete it, while another aspect of your instincts simply wakes it up as a defense mechanism.

Imagine yourself trying to tame a wild mare.

This is exactly what happens when jealousy wakes up in you. It is an emotional instinctual response which burns you because it wants to break free and find its natural expression.

Here are some key aspects to remember about your "jealousy weapon":

- **There is nothing wrong with you!**

  Jealousy is okay! It is your right to use it to defend your relationship.

- **Be the warrior**

  Instead of trying to suppress this natural emotional need, empower your fighting skills.

- **Protect your territory**

  Your territory is first your mind. This is where confidence is built. Don't let anyone put you down. Defend yourself fearlessly. Build empowering beliefs and give power to your emotional foundation.

- **Express! Don't suppress!**

  If you feel jealous about something or someone, dare to express it. Don't suppress. Look at these emotions straight in the eye. Jealousy is your fighting fire. This is what is behind it. It wakes up because there is competition. The dating scene is full of it. If you suppress it, you loose your power. Don't

www.vitalcoaching.com

suppress. Dare to express. It is a direct reflection of your inner power.

- **Jealousy is a weapon!**

  It was given to you. With any weapon, you need the right skills to be able to use it wisely. It is given to you. In fact, it is a gift. It is a gift of fire. Master this weapon. It is like a sword.

- **Your taming power**

  Your "taming power" is not control. It is what you use to master your jealousy. The fire of jealousy won't go away. It finds its way and "stabilizes" itself once you acknowledge its existence. You simply give it space and purpose.

- **Insecurity! The real challenge!**

  If you want to get rid of insecurity, you need to gain power. This is the real challenge. Jealousy is simply your best shot at defending your mind and relationship territory.

Your ultimate goal is to protect and preserve your relationship.

This is what you want, right?

You don't want to hurt your partner or anyone else.

This is not your goal.

However, your relationship can be under attack.

Jealousy is simply a defense mechanism.

Once you shift your mind set, you'll notice that what used to burn you does not burn you anymore.

www.vitalcoaching.com

There was a misunderstanding

The misunderstanding is about the territory of love:

In the dating scene, in love and relationships, you might tend to think that it is purely about love. It is not. <u>It is about power as well</u>.

These underlying power dynamics can generate tensions.

A jealousy response is related with a psychic balance of power between you and another woman.

You sometimes forget you need to fight.

Or you simply fight with ineffective tools.

An incoherent jealousy reaction is usually not the best response.

It can be very draining and self destructive.

You need to fight?

Simple!

Create a new level of power in your life.

Gain confidence and express your inner strength.

No one can threaten your mind space.

No one can threaten your confidence.

You have this basic power in you and no one can take it away from you.

<u>The first place to protect and preserve is your own mind</u>.

This is the core of your force.

The next area you want to protect is your relationship.

Being partners means that you look in the same direction.

You have a common vision.

www.vitalcoaching.com

You share synergy (= synchronized energy).

You are attuned with each other.

This is another aspect of your protective power: relationship synergy.

It is super effective and perfectly complements the "jealousy weapon"

It is never about you opposing him!

It's never about the fight between your two will powers.

The moment you set him free, you give him life and validation.

Then what? He gives it back to you.

The result? Infinite trust and respect!

Magic!

Who decided that control was okay in a relationship? It is not!

Use new tools. Use a new mind set and take your relationship to the next octave.

Think win-win always!

Think synergy, opening the space, freeing forces, liberating life force.

You can unleash the power of your relationship right now.

You can wake up to this new dimension of infinite trust.

www.vitalcoaching.com

Where to start?

Observe yourself.

Mastering your "jealousy weapon" is much vaster than that.

The long term goal is to have greater influence over what happens in your mind.

In fact it is a path of inner discovery and life mastery.

You can face jealousy, observe how it works and then manifest an extra quality which will simply tame this reaction in you.

It is not about erasing it or suppressing it.

It is about giving yourself other fighting tools.

These fighting tools are defense mechanisms which protect your self worth.

Jealousy is okay as long as you are not a victim of it.

It is okay to be jealous if you choose to.

When it is a "conscious game", it is no problem.

It can be a fun non invasive power game with your partner. You can play with it if you want to.

So, where to start?

Realize that this game is about accepting to go to battle.

It is a battle to protect your mind, personal space and relationship.

Use your will power and determination.

The battle field is your life and you are given the tools to succeed and master it!

www.vitalcoaching.com

How to protect yourself

The way to stop obsessive jealousy is to <u>gain extra power and confidence</u>.

When you have extra power, you mind feels stable and you are simply in control of what happens in it.

The goal is simple: <u>protect your mind space</u>.

Remember: <u>jealousy is your response to a threat</u>.

This threat is another woman. She challenges you and the relationship space.

If you don't want another woman's presence to threaten your emotional foundation, all you need is extra power and confidence.

You see, it is all about increasing your level of confidence and feeling secure.

The moment you create this aura of power in and around you, your jealousy simply expresses itself in a very different way: you are no longer a victim or slave of your jealousy.

You rather have the wisdom and skills to use it effectively exactly when needed.

Jealousy is not the enemy.

The real challenge is a power gap.

Competition

You are in competition with other women.

What is the game? Being number one in your partner's mind.

When you get jealous, this is the message you send out: "I want to be number one"

This is okay.

This is what goes on in relationships and in the dating scene.

There is love and attraction of course.

In love and dating dynamics, there is a psychic battle going on.

It is a battle of forces and energies.

People compete with each other. They compete for love and attention.

Jealousy is a battle strategy.

It is a "fighting" response.

The moment you feel pain in the form of jealousy, it is because your jealousy gets "trapped" in your system.

You don't manage to express this "fighting force" in an effective way.

It becomes an inner fire which consumes you.

Jealousy is a tool.

It is a "fighting skill" you can use.

What you don't want is that force to turn against you and consume your from within.

www.vitalcoaching.com

Shift to "battle" mode

Dating, relationships, social life are about love, right?

Well, love is of course in the centre of it but the dynamics between people are driven by something else as well: balance of power.

Jealousy is a defense mechanism.

In fact you have plenty of other defense responses which can work even better than jealousy's consuming fire.

First, realize that in any situation, there is always a battle of energies going on.

There is always a natural balance of power being established when two persons meet.

It is instinctual.

There is a balance of power happening straight away.

You will project jealousy the moment you feel threatened.

The less power you have, the more threatened you feel.

"Positive jealousy" on the other hand is a reaction you can control and master.

You decide when it happens and in what form.

Again, you are consumed by obsessive jealousy the moment you feel overpowered by an external force.

You feel insecure and obsessive jealousy is your best shot at reacting to this threat.

For jealousy to be effective, it has to reach its target.

What is your jealousy's target?

It is to preserve your connection with your partner.

www.vitalcoaching.com

How do you choose your best jealousy weapon?

Let's take a very specific example:

He keeps naked pictures of his ex and lies about it

In this example, he keeps naked pictures of his ex and says he doesn't. You know he is lying because you checked and found them amongst his personal belongings.

Let's check your options okay?

Here they are:

- **Dump him**

  This is a radical solution. You break up with him over this issue. There is no way back, no forgiveness or possibility for him to explain his behavior.

- **Destroy his red sport's car with your baseball bat**

  You express your anger freely!

- **Dialogue**

  You sit down and have a deep chat about it to try to understand why this is happening in your relationship, if it's okay, if he wants to do something about it, etc.

- **Confront him**

  You tell him about what you discovered, show him the pictures and give him space to explain or apologize.

- **Attack him**

  This is a more aggressive response. You use whatever words you feel like expressing, let your anger and frustration flow freely.

- **Threaten him**

www.vitalcoaching.com

"Unless you destroy these pictures, it's finished between us!".
"I give you a week to shift your attitude or I'm done with
you!"

- **Educate him**

  You sit down and explain to him how this makes you feel. You
  show him a better way to validate you and stand in this
  relationship with you.

- **Attack his ex**

  You call her and tell her to stay away from your partner.

- **Destroy these pictures**

  You trash these pictures, burn them or cut them in small
  pieces.

- **Change the way you relate to him**

  You realize that he is not as committed to you as you thought
  he was. You decide to step a bit back and slightly disinvest
  yourself from the relationship. You take steps to protect
  yourself in the future.

- **Tolerate it**

  You accept it and realize that you can actually live with it.

- **Embrace it**

  You realize that no one is perfect and that it's with you he
  decides to be. You decide to embrace all aspects of his
  personality rather than trying to change him.

- **Enjoy it**

  You enjoy it because you realize it's with you he decides to be.
  This connection with his ex does in fact refresh your
  relationship because it makes him realize the value of what
  you two share.

Okay!

This is only a sample of your potential strategies.

www.vitalcoaching.com

You can of course ad extra ones if other ideas come to your mind.

If you want to throw yourself in a battle <u>you better be clear about your target</u> and understand that <u>a certain strategy will tend to bring a specific result</u>.

Most of the times <u>you can easily foresee what your actions will create</u>.

What is striking as well is that you do have many choices, not just one!

The next step is very simple: <u>choose the strategies which best fit your needs</u>.

Suppose that you face a similar type of challenge in your relationship.

Write down again or print this set of strategies and ad as well a few more if you feel that some are not mentioned.

Here is your list again:

- **Dump him**
- **Destroy his red sport's car with your baseball bat**
- **Dialogue**
- **Confront him**
- **Attack him**
- **Threaten him**
- **Educate him**
- **Attack his ex**
- **Destroy these pictures**
- **Change the way you relate to him**
- **Tolerate it**
- **Embrace it**

- **Enjoy it**

In that case, you have 13 possible strategies.

The next step is to choose the strategy (weapon) which is the most adapted to your situation. You do this for instance by giving each strategy a mark between 0% and 100% (0%=no use   100%=best)

This gives you a set of strategies which can look like:

- **Dump him**	**0%**
- **Destroy his red sport's car**	**0%**
- **Dialogue**	**5%**
- **Confront him**	**95%**
- **Attack him**	**0%**
- **Threaten him**	**0%**
- **Educate him**	**5%**
- **Attack his ex**	**0%**
- **Destroy these pictures**	**5%**
- **Change the way you relate to him**	**5%**
- **Tolerate it**	**5%**
- **Embrace it**	**5%**
- **Enjoy it**	**5%**

Use your instinct! Just write down the mark that comes first! It is usually the right one!

In this example, you see clearly that the best strategy is to confront him, right?

The next step is to find a way of confronting him which is really constructive for your couple.

By the way, every situation is slightly different.

www.vitalcoaching.com

In that case, confronting him was our first choice.

It does not need to be that way though! This is just an example. It might be totally different for you.

In your unique situation, you might realize that another strategy might be a better fit.

It will depend on your personality, the dynamics that you two create and the specific details of your situation.

For instance, you might prefer a more aggressive attitude like destroying his self esteem by exposing him in public at his next birthday party (really nasty! ☺).

If you are really open minded, you might choose for the opposite strategy which is to enjoy every aspect of what he does rather than trying to change him.

You simply realize that these pictures are no real threat to your relationship. They might even give you some ideas.

This is simply the process of choosing the best "jealousy weapon" which fits your unique situation.

You might as well choose for a combination of actions like confronting him and booking your next holiday without him for instance.

www.vitalcoaching.com

Easy to shift jealousy? How come women get stacked with it?

Excellent question!

Most women tend to stay stacked with this issue because they don't see a valid enough reason to change.

For those who genuinely want to change but don't find a way to, what they miss is simply an effective strategy.

Suppose you are a jealous woman. Your first instinct is to try to suppress your jealousy response.

It's like trying to put a lid on it!

It usually does not work!

The first step is to understand more about jealousy dynamics, how they originate, why they are there in the first place, the role they play in your love life, etc.

Once you have a greater understanding of the jealousy dynamics, you respectfully reorient the power behind your jealousy and use it in a more effective way.

You learn to communicate with your partner more effectively.

You discover extra sources of power in you.

You reframe your mind sets and reposition the way you stand in your relationship.

Basically, you master that power and energy!

You don't suppress it!

This is why the average woman does not usually tap into these techniques without a little guidance and support.

It is because it takes time and energy to discover all that by yourself.

www.vitalcoaching.com

I am convinced that you know already everything you will read in this book. A part of you knows it but you are not aware of it.

All these instincts we talk about are deeply buried in your subconscious mind and we simply bring them to the surface so that you can start using them.

If you prefer reinventing the wheel by yourself, you are welcome to go ahead. I do believe that if you focus on it for a few months or more, you will eventually discover some of the techniques and ideas I am about to share with you.

Even if you really dive in it by yourself without this material, you will only unveil a fraction of what you will discover in this book.

The question is: do you have three months? Do you have the time and energy to do all that by yourself or do you prefer taking the direct short cut I am sharing with you.

As soon as you see the strategies I talk about, the path to master your jealousy is crystal clear!

Again, it is not that complicate. You simply need the right set of strategies.

www.vitalcoaching.com

I have always been the jealous type

When you say "I've always been the jealous type", you limit yourself.

If this is the case, it is time to change your mind pattern and ideas.

Obsessive jealousy consumes and destroys relationships.

Right now, it is consuming you and wasting your energy into useless emotional loops.

A part of you defends your jealousy.

A part of you even likes it or is proud of it.

Now, you are defending the very source of your pain.

This is where the conflict lies.

For the last 10 years of your life, you lived with this pattern in your mind and probably accepted it as YOUR identity.

I 100% disagree.

Jealousy is a mind set.

It is like a shirt you put on and enjoy.

What you need to do now is find a new mind set which will give you greater satisfaction.

You need to do two things:

- The first one is getting rid of the obsessive jealousy pattern.
- The second one is finding a new mind set which works better.

If you remove your "jealousy shirt", you need to find a new identity.

The question is:

What is the slogan you will write on your shirt?

www.vitalcoaching.com

What is the quality which is 100 times better than obsessive jealousy and which solves all your dilemmas?

The answer is "Trust".

Right now, you are constricting your partner's space.

What you do when you get over jealous is keeping him on a leash.

True! I am serious.

I don't see there an expression of love.

I see an expression of control and inner fears.

This is what I see when you are obsessively jealous.

Does this generate harmony?

No!

Is this an expression of love?

No!

Then what is it?

It is an expression of power and control.

In fact, by being jealous you kill the very essence of what you love in him: his freedom, smile, openness, joy and life force.

All these qualities are what you are supposed to protect in him.

When you get over jealous, you do exactly the opposite: you kill them.

This is what happens.

If you love somebody, set them free (that's from "Sting...")

How do you set someone free?

By reaffirming your trust, respect and love.

When you do this, you empower him.

www.vitalcoaching.com

You give him strength, confidence.

So, what shirt will it be this morning?

The one which hurts and says "Jealousy" in screaming letters, or will it be the new pattern of "TRUST".

You do have the choice!

www.vitalcoaching.com

How can you change if you have a bad jealousy problem?

That's the whole point, right?

Change!

The key is reconditioning!

When you get used to a certain emotional pattern like jealousy, you keep on doing it over and over again until you instruct your mind to respond in a different way.

Now, most women give up on even trying because they don't know how or where to start!

Imagine: you spend 20 or 30 years of your life expressing a pattern which does not work!

It hurts you! It hurts your husband or boyfriend! It destroys your relationships...

All that because you did not find an exit door for that specific emotion.

I don't blame you! It is a challenge to shift a jealousy pattern when you don't know where to start.

www.vitalcoaching.com

Can you ever change if you are the jealous type?

Of course you can!!!

Jealousy is a pattern you can influence and change!

It is simply an emotional reaction. Now, the only reason why you choose a jealous reaction is because you don't have other tools or other skills.

If I ask you: what is the alternative to a jealous response, I bet that you will have difficulties even imagining what it looks like.

It does not mean that a non jealous response does not exist! It simply means that you did not manifest it yet.

An emotional response is like a shirt you put on. If you have only one shirt, you will wear it all the time.

If you know you have a few, you will select the one you prefer, right?

If you have only one card, you keep on playing that one over and over again simply because you have no other.

So, to shift a jealousy pattern you need other options. You need to develop and train new skills!

www.vitalcoaching.com

Isn't being jealousy a bit like being emotionally immature?

Yes! It can be, but not always.

When you grow emotionally as a woman, you learn to master the jealousy patterns.

The reason women fall into jealousy traps is simply because of lack of skills. That's all!

Sometimes, you might believe that creating jealousy drama actually tells that you care.

In fact, it rather shows that you are trapped.

Especially if you or anyone else gets hurt in the process.

If you do express jealousy and don't feel limited by this emotion, it means that you do master it to a certain extent, which is very good.

If you and your partner are happy, it usually shows that you are doing something right.

It is not jealousy itself which is immature. It is rather the way it might be used.

If you feel enslaved by an emotion you don't like, that's the sign that something is unfulfilled and that you have room for improvement.

See jealousy as a weapon or tool you can master. That's the final goal.

www.vitalcoaching.com

I like being jealous! - Is there something wrong with me?

Not at all!

Expressing your jealousy in a wise way is an expression of your power!

What you need to check is:

- How does this impact on your partner's life?
- Are you emotionally abusive?
- Are you limiting him and controlling his life?
- Is he happy?
- Did he threaten to leave you if you don't stop?

These are the questions you need to answer.

Jealousy is a power.

Are you abusing this power or are you using it with love and respect?

I am not here to judge any of your actions.

If you and your partner are happy, it shows that you are doing something right.

Now, if he gets hurt by over controlling or demanding attitudes, it is usually the sign that you are going one step too far.

If it is the case, deciding to do something about it is your choice, no one else's.

www.vitalcoaching.com

My girlfriend is super jealous! - She thinks it's just normal!

Many women will keep on using jealousy or control until their partner tells them to stop.

Obviously this bothers them, right?

The truth is that his life belongs to him. He has the right to decide for himself what he wants.

Even when you get married, believing that this gives you the right to tell him what to do or not is a mistake.

So, why do some women believe that it's okay to limit their partner's freedom?

The question now is: what to do about it?

Any time he claims his freedom back, he can face resistance.

He might go to battle and design new boundaries with you.

Now, you need to be smart with this.

Claiming his freedom is his right as a human being.

He has the right to decide for himself what he wants or doesn't want.

The moment he expresses that power and rejects his partner's authority, he is backed up by his own spirit and a force which is much vaster than himself.

Ultimately, this has to do with human dignity.

www.vitalcoaching.com

Make sure he does not leave you over jealousy issues

Guys do break up with women over jealousy issues.

If you don't want this to happen, you need to take action and get rid of whatever limits him in your relationship.

You might think: "Well, if I give him total freedom, isn't he going to cheat on me?"

What do you think?

I think it actually works the other way round!

The more you limit him, the more he'll want to run away with another woman!

Your new attitude is called trust!

You replace jealousy, possessiveness and control by a refreshing quality of trust!

Of course, you'll have a conversation in the early stages of your relationship where you define exactly what commitment means to both of you.

You could say:

"I could not stand you cheating on me. I know that if it happens, we are done! I have no problem with you having female friends as long as I know you are not intimate with them. I need to be number one in your life..."

This is called setting up boundaries. You tell him what you feel is okay or not.

You talk about this a couple of times before you fully commit to each other.

He might give you a similar set of boundaries.

Once this is done, you have to set each other free!

www.vitalcoaching.com

What does this mean exactly?

You simply don't limit each other.

No control!

No demands!

Respect + Trust!

Men break up with women over one key reason: they feel limited in the relationship they are in.

When he breaks up, he says things like: "I need space!"

What he is in fact saying is: "I can't breathe! I feel limited! I am not myself anymore!"

Got it?

If you don't want this to happen to him, you want to position yourself in a way which is freeing him, not limiting him.

Are you afraid of giving him freedom? I bet you are!!!

Trusting someone is always a risk you take!

Now, trusting turns into the most exhilarating experience when you express it!

The complicity and connection which can be born from expressing that trust is absolutely thrilling.

www.vitalcoaching.com

How to respond to jealousy triggers

When you get jealous, there is always a trigger!

The first step is to identify the trigger and the situation where jealousy pops up.

If you analyze your jealousy challenges, you will notice that you can usually summarize them to 2 or 3 key relationship situations:

- It might be his ex calling.
- His attitude when you go out.
- He taking off to the gym in the evening.
- His female colleague texting him when he is with you.
- Etc.

Now, identify the top 2 or 3 situations which trigger jealousy in your case.

Write them down!

You now have a clear target, right?

The goal is to shift the dynamics in that specific situation.

You can either:

- Educate him and get him to shift his behavior.

or

- Shift the way you respond to that specific trigger.

This last option will usually be the way to go.

Why? Because that's what usually gives you the best long lasting results.

What we just did is very simple:

We reduced the jealousy challenge to a couple of situations you can easily analyze and oversea.

www.vitalcoaching.com

Instead of saying: "I am a jealous woman and I don't know what to do..."

You are now saying: "I feel uncomfortable when I see him having a chat with his ex... How can I shift my attitude so that this no longer bothers me?"

See what happened? We made it very specific!

This simplifies and reduces the challenge to a size you can easily handle!

www.vitalcoaching.com

Why getting rid of unwanted jealousy is so thrilling!

Have you ever been in a dream where you feel trapped?

Do you remember the exciting relief when you wake up?

You realize that there is a way out!

This is how it feels to solve the jealousy riddle!

Of course, you don't want to look at it when you believe that there is no way out or that you have to go through 5 years of therapy to solve it.

Now, imagine what happens when you realize that jealousy challenges can be rapidly solved without you losing your power!

Do you feel this clear freshness waking up in your mind?

You suddenly perceive a whole new set of possibilities for you and your partner.

Open doors!

That's how it feels!

Part of you might not believe that this is possible?

Well! It is!

I am not fooling you around!

This is your life and the challenge you face is a big deal! Really! I am aware of it!

This is important!

It takes some courage to trust and believe in yourself!

I don't know you but I believe in you!

I believe in your power and infinite potential!

www.vitalcoaching.com

I know that because you set up your mind to it you are easily winning this battle.

And guess what?

Once you achieve this specific victory, you can focus on new aspects of your life which really matter.

There is a whole world of possibilities for your refreshed couple.

Grab this opportunity now and don't let go! This is your chance!

www.vitalcoaching.com

How women give away their power and try getting it back

The more power you give away to your boyfriend or husband, the more you try to get it back through jealousy, insecurity or controlling patterns.

See your individual base as an entity.

You feel secure when you are in control of that base.

The day you get into a relationship you often give too much of that power to your new partner.

You simply give him the right to have control over your actions, thoughts, time frame, attitudes, etc.

This power transfer is mainly unconscious.

You believe it is right to make concessions and go with what he wants rather than what you want.

This is how many women lose their power!

They simply give it up!

You end up giving him the control seat in your life.

Now, what are the consequences of that?

On your side, it tends to generate insecurity and greater desire to control him.

This gets expressed in jealousy patterns as well.

The reason why you want to control his life is because you simply want to gain back what you gave him.

Imagine that you own a certain "volume" of controlling power.

When you are single, you express this in your own life.

You use this controlling power to protect your freedom and stay in charge of what is yours.

www.vitalcoaching.com

Now, when you get into a relationship and you allow him to step in and control some aspects of your own personal life (like career choices, activities, food choices, clothes, social life, etc.) you end up with an extra unused reserve of controlling power.

The most natural way to express this controlling power is often to project it into his life and try to control some aspects of his existence, get over jealous or very insecure.

This is when your couple gets in trouble.

Realize that you express insecurity towards him simply because you feel you are no longer in charge of your own life.

Therefore you start relying on him to provide you with this security.

If he decides to go on a date with his ex, you end up with a big power gap and feelings of anxiousness and insecurity.

It happens because you gave your power away earlier and don't have the resources now to emotionally protect yourself.

When he goes on a date with his ex or flirts with other women, you end up with no control over either you or him.

Can you see these power dynamics?

They are very organic and instinctual.

It is an energy equation which needs to be balanced.

So, what is the solution to all that?

It is quite simple!

If you don't want insecurity, controlling patterns or jealousy to rise in your being, stay in charge of your life!

Don't give him the control seat!

Don't delegate your power and don't let him choose what is right for you!

You need to stay in charge of your own life!

www.vitalcoaching.com

This is a decision you take in the very early stages of your relationship.

Don't give up your power!

The next question is:

How do you build up a relationship without giving up your power?

Is it even possible?

Of course it is!

www.vitalcoaching.com

Justified jealousy and when it's okay to express it

In some situations, expressing your jealousy is very good.

Suppose that you are out with him and he starts talking about his ex.

In fact, it happened many times before.

It became a pattern.

He praises what she does or what they did in the past.

It feels draining for you!

Should you say something?

Of course you should!

"I don't really want to hear about your ex. Is this okay with you? Thank you"

This is called a boundary.

It protects the time you have together.

When you educate him or express a boundary, you need to be firm and consistent.

You might need as well to repeat the same message a few times until he truly gets it.

You can take a special moment later to tell him exactly why you no longer want to hear about his ex.

He talking about an ex again and again is one example.

Here are some more situations which can trigger a justified jealousy response:

- He keeps a portrait of him and his ex which everyone can see in the house where you live together.

- He talks a lot about a specific female friend.
- He picks up a call and spends 30 min on the phone when you are out having dinner together.
- He frequently cancels dates with you at the last minute because of work.
- Etc.

As you can see, not all these situations would be called "jealousy" issues.

What they have in common though is that, your partner's attitude is tactless and you can educate him.

Some even more obvious justified jealousy responses happen if he cheats or lies to you.

You can as well express positive jealousy towards a woman who definitely comes too close to him and does not respect your couple.

The first question to ask is:

"In this situation, is jealousy justified or not?"

In 95% of the cases, jealousy is unjustified.

It means that you might tend to overreact, mistrust and blow up a potentially nice evening without good reason.

This is why most of the female jealousy strategies are focused on shifting your response rather than educating him.

Use positive jealousy and educate him only in some isolated and exceptional situations.

Trying to educate him must represent less than 5% of the conversations you have with him.

Why? Because that's the maximum he can usually take!

Every now and then (max once a month!) you have an opportunity and a need to ask him to shift a behavior that bothers you.

Remember that educating him happens only in some exceptional cases!

www.vitalcoaching.com

In most situations, shifting your own response and respecting his freedom is what works best!

If you overused jealousy and control in the past, forget even totally about trying to educate him on anything for a while, at least until you deal with your own issues!

MIRROR TACTICS! - Do EXACTLY what he does!

I call these "Mirror tactics".

Suppose that he gets too flirty with a girl at a social event.

Instead of going after him, find a guy and do the same. Flirt!

Make it obvious and don't hold back.

This will most probably trigger a reaction on his side.

You see, most men will defend their right to be open and free with anyone until you start being open and free too.

That's when it hits them.

They feel it too: the insecurity!

They feel the jealousy emotions kicking in.

Mirroring his behavior is one of the best ways to let him see how it feels to be in your shoes.

You don't pressure him. You don't express your jealousy to him.

Instead, you do EXACTLY what he does.

If this triggers a conversation and he gets angry with you for flirting with another man, here is what you say next:

"So, you don't like it when I flirt with another guy?"

"Why not?"

"How does that make you feel?"

"I thought you too were having a good time with that girl tonight"

"Would you say that we were both engaging in flirting or connecting with someone else?"

www.vitalcoaching.com

Jealousy – How to deal with it – For women

"So, if I stop flirting with other guys, does that mean you have to stop flirting with other girls too?"

Now, that's usually when it hits him!

This simple realization will often trigger the behavior change you want in him.

He will do it because he knows that he doesn't like it when the situation is reversed.

He respects you.

He doesn't want to hurt you.

Now, he knows BY EXPERIENCE how his flirting with another girl makes YOU feel.

Next time you go out, you might feel him staying CONSCIOUSLY closer to you out of his OWN choice.

There was no demand! There was no pressure.

Women come to me ALL THE TIME with this type of breakthrough when they use these mirror tactics.

They work amazingly well to get him to shift a behavior in his own terms.

In most cases, what's interesting is that if you tried to "force" that behavior change on him, it would probably trigger a fight.

Now, because it is his decision and he came to that conclusion by himself, that's a totally different story.

He embraces that choice rather than resenting it!

The other essential point for you to understand is that when he shifts a behavior, YOU trigger that positive change in him by NOT challenging him on this issue and GIVING him space to change it IF he wants to on his own time and terms.

Very impressive when this happens.

Please email me your success story when you get such break through, ok?

www.vitalcoaching.com

Would love to hear it!

http://vitalcoaching.com/contact.htm

Call me instead of unloading your insecurities on him

Once you start working with these jealousy files you will see that most of the strategies to handle the situations you face are already written and in a way, you are already using them.

All you might need now is someone who helps you stay focused when delusional or unjustified fears kick in.

The worst you can do is to go to him for help when this happens.

Remember that he's not your therapist.

It's not his job to reassure you systematically, especially if these episodes are frequent.

So, here is the strategy I want to share with you:

Call me!

My number is on my site:

http://vitalcoaching.com/contact.htm

Here is what I suggest you do:

Next time, you have an insecurity or jealousy episode, pick up the phone and call me for an unscheduled power kick!

If you get my voice mail, leave me a message and I'll call you back as soon as I can.

It is that simple.

I give you a safe space to share your fears and we'll check together the best strategy to handle this.

What I give you is more power.

This is not therapy, ok! I think you are perfectly fine! This is about performance and life mastery and this is EXACTLY what I can help you with.

www.vitalcoaching.com

I have a few clients I coach that way on jealousy issues and we often have non scheduled sessions when they feel challenged.

I might speak with them maybe a couple times a month.

Sometimes, I don't hear from them for a few weeks or months.

This is it!

The results I see happening in these women are amazing.

The advantage of having me on call that way is that you don't bring these issues to your boyfriend. In a way you keep him out of it which REALLY protects your couple.

In my opinion, this is by far the best way to go...

I made it very easy and totally affordable for you.

Check it out on my site:

http://vitalcoaching.com/coaching.htm

www.vitalcoaching.com

How to stay cool always! No matter what he does!

Staying cool is an attitude you train!

You prepare yourself for the absolute worst and imagine how you would react if you were the coolest person on this planet.

What would you do?

What would you say?

Expressing insecurities in relationships is a lack of emotional maturity.

It simply says that your mind and personal power are not strong enough yet!

Yes! The goal is to always be in a positive and uplifting state of mind no matter what.

If you go out together and already feel what could trigger a fight, you prepare yourself before it even happens.

You DECIDE not to respond before the situation even arises.

I agree with you, it takes focus and determination to achieve just that.

But guess what?

This is part of your life mastery training.

This is how you become a better person and grow character.

This is how you become a partner he enjoys and wants to spend his time with.

To your power!

www.vitalcoaching.com

Part 5 – Right boundaries

Build up peace! Give him space to relax!

When your irritation threshold is very low, your partner walks on egg shells all the time!

He can't relax!

He must be ready for an attack and be on the defensive all the time!

This is exhausting after a while!

You simply need to increase your tolerance level and give him space to relax.

Creating peace and harmony in your relationship is something you do consciously by choice!

Defend his freedom

If you want to remember one thing from this material, this is it!

Defend his freedom!

Defend his happiness!

Defend his rights!

If you are looking for a new way of expressing your power, this is the exact shift you need to make.

It is not overprotecting!

It is not being afraid for him!

It is stimulating and defending what you care for the most in him:

His joy and pleasure to be alive!

If you crush that, you crush part of yourself!

When you express jealousy, you use your "controlling power".

When you defend his freedom, you use your "protective power".

What is the difference?

Controlling power limits!

Protective power opens doors!

This is the exact way to express your power in the future.

You are not dropping your power, you are expressing it differently!

There are two key ways you can approach nature: as a hunter or as a defender!

The same applies to men!

You have two ways you can love him:

www.vitalcoaching.com

- By closing your arms around him and limiting him.

Or

- Opening your arms around him and giving him space and freedom.

These two approaches are totally different.

So many people are trapped in the first model!

It is much more challenging to love unconditionally and sponsor his freedom and destiny no matter what.

If you are looking for a new way to use your infinite source of power, this is it!

Protect, sponsor and defend his freedom!

This is the true alternative to jealousy patterns.

Ask yourself:

- Do you want him to be with you because you force him to?

Or

- Do you want him to be with you because he is free and chooses to?

By the way, you can replace the word "freedom" by "happiness", "destiny line", "joy", "pleasure to be alive" or anything you feel inspired to.

Defend his freedom!

How he will react to pressure and demands

If you say something like:

"I don't want you to be so open with everyone when we go to social events! I don't like it! It makes me VERY uncomfortable!"

What's the usual emotional response to that?

Will he be cool and say something like:

"Sure, I didn't realize I was crossing the line - I'll be happy to change my behavior - What you want is very important to me."

Or will he say something like:

"Are you telling me what to do now? Whaou! I can't believe this! You actually used to like it when I was fun and outgoing! Now you want me to become the wall paper guy who says nothing? Why on earth do you ask me to do something like that?"

You guessed right!

In most cases, HE WILL REBEL!

He will fight back, attack you and defend his right to do whatever he wants.

Why is that?

Why is it that he doesn't see your point?

Here is the answer:

It is because in a subtle way, you are not just asking him to change, you are as well:

- Accusing him
- Limiting his freedom
- Demanding
- Projecting an emotionally loaded request
- Telling him that he's not good enough
- Saying that he's doing something wrong

www.vitalcoaching.com

- Etc.

How do YOU react when someone attacks you?

Do you just give in or do you fight back?

Do you engage in a constructive feed back conversation or do you cave in and retreat?

See the point?

There is a way of communicating with him which works 100 times better than demands!

Here we go:

"I face a challenge and I don't know what to do about it... Want to help me with that? What do you suggest?"

What happened there?

You asked for his opinion and input.

You design a solution TOGETHER!

That's a totally different story, right?

Here is the line you can use next time you have a feed back chat with him:

"What do you suggest?"

Don't use your controlling power to limit him

If you have lots of power...

If professionally and materially, you have a solid base are in charge of your existence...

Being in that place does involve control over what is yours.

Now, when you are in a relationship, there is a natural risk to use the same type of controlling force on him.

Jealousy patterns are an expression of your controlling power.

The thing is that this controlling power can precisely kill what you love the most.

You know that already of course.

You don't want to alienate your partner, isolate him or make him feel miserable.

Of course you won't go that way.

Imagine just for a second that you would express all the jealousy patterns and controlling impulses that raise in your mind, it would be a nightmare for him, right?

What does this tell you?

That this controlling power is dangerous for your relationship.

It is literally a fire that can burn down your couple.

You know that already. I am saying this to reinforce a fact you are already familiar with.

The key idea is to use your power wisely!

It usually means PROTECTING MORE and CONTROLLING LESS.

www.vitalcoaching.com

Use your protective force rather than control

You see positive expressions of protective power all the time in society!

It shows up when:

- A boss gives you space to be creative at your job.
- A mother watches her child playing in the park.
- You let a dog run freely while keeping an eye on what it does.
- We redirect the flow of a river so that a village doesn't get hit with the next storm.
- Etc.

In all these expressions, people are STILL using their power!

It is not control.

It is protection!

- You don't limit the employee's creativity.
- You don't hold the child by the hand.
- You don't keep the dog on the leash.
- You don't stop the river from flowing.

What's the result?

LIFE FLOWS!

It's not being stopped or limited!

That's one of the core distinctions you can make when using your power in life.

How much control is REALLY needed to keep you safe?

Do you need 5 locks or just one?

Do you really need a high fence?

See the point?

In your relationship, controlling power is a joy killer!

www.vitalcoaching.com

It destroys spontaneity and complicity.

When partners use it, what they really say is:

"I don't trust you! I don't think you are grown up enough to make your own decisions!"

Using control on your partner usually means SERIOUS TROUBLE!

What's the alternative if you don't want to lose your power?

Well, you still use your power but in a different way.

When dealing with relationship boundaries, you will say things like:

- "Looks like this girl was really into you" rather than "I don't want you to speak with her again!"

If you see him chatting with another woman, you approach them and say:

- "Who is your friend" rather than "Do you always need to flirt with girls like that when we are out???"

If he looks fresh and excited when taking off to the gym, you'll say:

- "Whaou! You look like a rock star - I am so glad I am the one you have sex with" rather than "You are not planning to go to the gym dressed like that, are you?!"

These subtle distinctions are essential if you want to really connect with your partner.

Protective power? He'll enjoy it!

Controlling or limiting power? He'll rebel!

What's your choice?

www.vitalcoaching.com

His energy is precisely what attracts you to him

A man's happiness is VERY precious.

When I interview women on this topic, they often say that what got them attracted to their boyfriend are his smile and radiance.

It is the fact that he looked confident, happy, fun and outgoing.

That's a trait you DON'T want your boyfriend to lose! Believe me!

That's what brings joy to your relationship and makes it fun to be with him.

The moment you kill that, you destroy what you care for the most.

You need to manage your jealousy without destroying these qualities in him.

As a life partner, your job is to protect his freedom and happiness, not to destroy them!

So, how do you manage that tricky challenge?

You trust him and tell him what the TRUE boundary is.

The true boundary is: "Don't get intimate with another woman - If you do, I'm out"

That's usually the deal breaker in relationships.

95% of couples agree with this subtle and often unspoken agreement.

The other 5% of couples will have an open relationship or some higher degree of sexual freedom.

Listen, when he's happy and even flirty, what bothers you is not so much what you see, it is the potential of what COULD follow up.

You get jealous because you IMAGINE what COULD happen next.

www.vitalcoaching.com

Of course if you see him flirting with another girl, it might bother you a bit.

But what really gets to you is if they establish a connection that can lead to something else.

He needs to know what your EXACT boundary is:

"No intimacy with another woman"

Once he knows, give him space and trust him!

Being clingy or desperate is a big turn off for men

When you are extremely possessive and jealous, you sound very desperate.

It is a huge turn off for him.

Having to constantly feed a woman's emotional needs can be very demanding for a guy.

It creates pressure and limits him within the relationship.

The alternative is to stay in your own power.

Stay in charge of your own life.

In most cases, the best way to create long term harmony in the relationship is to maintain a strong personal individual base.

When you "abandon" yourself in a relationship, you become very vulnerable.

Stay in control of your life.

Go beyond the "exclusively passionate dream".

Stay awake!

Keep your survival and fighting skills alive.

If you transfer all your power to your partner and simply rely on him for validation and security, this kills part of your self worth and personal power.

Don't give up your personal independence and own destiny line.

No need to sacrifice yourself.

When you challenge yourself, you empower your own vehicle.

You don't wait for your partner to show up.

You go on and follow up with your life.

www.vitalcoaching.com

Action is life force.

Action is what gives you extra confidence and deletes unwanted jealousy.

Join forces with your partner, sure, <u>but don't give up your individual identity</u>.

Make sure that you are able to stand on your own any time.

This immensely empowers your relationship on the long term.

Are you committed or not?

If you are a jealous woman, this is probably the first question to ask yourself.

Why?

Because the only reason that justifies jealousy is if you need to protect the territory of your relationship.

This is how the jealousy instinct was created in the first place.

If you are non committed, being jealous is a waste of time and energy.

You try to protect something that does not exist.

On top of that, you do violate his most basic human right: his right for freedom!!!

Conclusion?

In that situation, being jealous is a waste of your precious time!

Is excessive jealousy emotional abuse?

Definitely yes!!!

A man is emotionally abused when a woman tries to control his life, steals his freedom, limits him, and tells him what to think, wear or feel!!!

These are definitely abusive situations.

How bad are these patterns? It simply depends on the intensity!

If you are a woman and discover abusive patterns like these, you need to educate yourself and shift these behaviors.

Is a little jealousy good in a relationship?

Of course it is!

The question is not whether or not you are allowed to express jealousy.

The real question is: are you in control of your jealousy or does your jealousy control you?

Jealousy is simply a tool!!! It is a weapon.

If you know how to use it effectively it will positively impact on your relationship.

Now, if you see that your controlling attitudes destroy your couple, it means that you misuse your jealousy weapon.

You destroy what you try to protect.

Men love it when they see their partners really caring for them.

Being a bit jealous here and there is a good way of showing that you care.

But!!!! It's essential that you stay on top of that emotion and play your jealousy card as a game.

You use it when you want and can withdraw it whenever you want.

This is the real skill you need to develop.

Don't be the slave of your jealousy! Be its master!

www.vitalcoaching.com

Why does he try to make you jealous?

Most of the times, it is a teasing game.

Nothing serious.

It is a way of flirting.

It is a seduction game.

It is a good sign.

It is a sign that there is complicity and that he wants to seduce you.

If you are offended by it, it blows up the game.

Instead, play the game:

Make him jealous as well.

If he is really trying to hurt you, it is of course another story.

Can you see that?

Making you jealous is his way of wanting your attention.

If you do this to a man, it is a seduction game.

It is part of the flirting game.

You make him come closer and then playfully reject him.

You do this to wake up his desire and even to stimulate sexual tension between the two of you.

It is a game.

Enjoy it!

www.vitalcoaching.com

Power dynamics in social situations

Check these two situations:

Situation 1

Suppose you see a woman looking at your partner.

You are prettier than her.

You have a better job and there is no way your partner would be interested in flirting with her.

She has less power than you do.

Will you feel threatened?

Maybe a little, but insecurity won't consume you.

You might feel some jealousy waking up as a superficial emotional reaction.

This woman has less power than you have.

This "threat" does not reach you.

You feel safe.

You feel strong.

It is a balance of power.

You win because you have more power.

Situation 2

www.vitalcoaching.com

Now imagine the same situation with your partner flirting with a girl who seems to have it all: career, looks, confidence.

You might feel your partner getting turned on by this woman.

They obviously link.

She impacts on your self confidence in a very different way.

Because she has more power, you tend to feel insecure and threatened.

If she gives him her business card, you'll feel a "mark" of her presence in your partner's mind.

You will react to it.

This mark is an invasion of your "relationship's space".

You feel her presence within the walls of your relationship.

Can you see that?

Two very different power dynamics.

In the second situation, she has her "foot" inside the wall. This gives her extra power and it consumes you.

She has a link with your partner.

This creates suffering for you because it is an invasion of your relationship's space.

It is always a battle of energies.

Sometimes you win the battle and you are fine.

Sometimes you lose in the balance of power and it consumes you.

The reason jealousy wakes up in you is because of this conflict for power, attention and energy.

To deal with such situations you need a battle strategy. You need effective emotional tools to deal with it.

www.vitalcoaching.com

Sometimes you fight with a "ghost", a threat which does not really exist physically.

Sometimes you are challenged by a real person who invades your relationship's space.

Establish complicity with your partner

He is on your side, right?

A social event is an occasion to have fun.

So why could you feel insecure and get jealous?

You can get jealous because there are power dynamics involved.

People compete with each other in a subconscious way.

The result? You might feel challenged.

So will your partner and so will your relationship.

If you are ready for battle and feel in power, external threats will simply bounce on the surface of your couple's mind.

If another woman challenges your relationship's space, will she weaken your link with your partner?

She won't if you two stay accomplices.

A simple wink, a look to your partner can mean a lot.

It can mean:

"We both know what is happening and it is okay to play the game, this is not threatening what we share"

A girl flirts with your man? Play the game.

It is okay if you know you are accomplices even in that.

How do you build up complicity?

You build up complicity by openly talking about this type of situations with your partner:

- "What do we do when this happens?"
- "How do we feel?"
- "What is our strategy?"

www.vitalcoaching.com

Open communication with your partner is the key.

You have a common goal: it is to empower your relationship and have fun at the same time.

Social events like a friend's party often have a "challenging dimension" in them.

You'll feel fine if you have a battle strategy to handle these challenges.

Complicity shifts everything: it gives trust, power and confidence.

In fact you establish an effective "battle strategy" with him.

If there is a threat you know he is on your side and you are on his.

You join forces and this protects you and the couple even if he chats with another woman.

Creating complicity is a relationship skill.

It is one of the key strategies to transmute unwanted jealousy.

Complicity is this powerful pillar in your relationship.

It is the perfect alternative to unwanted jealousy.

You create harmony. You create trust. You generate power.

You empower the relationship by creating this strong bond.

It is an inner contract which says:

"We stand in this together and we stay awake. We know what is going on and this does not alter the trust and confidence we have for each other."

www.vitalcoaching.com

If he talks a lot about other women

Educate your partner!

Talking about other women when he is in a relationship or on a date with you is a lack of dating skills.

It is a lack of tact.

You don't need to hear that. The fantasies which go on in his mind are okay as long as he doesn't picture them for you.

Tell him! Design a new boundary in your relationship.

Tell him until he gets it and shifts his attitude.

Going on a date with you is about you, the two of you, not him and someone else.

It is your right to establish a new boundary.

Tell him: "I would rather talk about something else. Is it okay with you?"

If you enjoy his love stories, it is different of course.

However, if this wakes up unwanted jealousy in you, tell him you don't want to hear that.

Simple and direct!

When you are on a date, it is nice to feel valued.

It is about what you two have in common.

Educate him on that.

It is okay.

Repeat the message until he gets it.

www.vitalcoaching.com

He looks at other women when we go out

When this happens with your partner, rebuild complicity.

Say something like: "Helloooo!!! You want her for breakfast?" when he checks another girl.

It's your way of participating in this and playing jealous without being consumed by it.

Express it in a humorous or teasing way.

It is a very effective way to educate him and let him know how his behavior makes you feel.

This takes away any tension and gets your message through.

You can as well reverse the game and point your finger towards a nice hank and say:

"Hmmm.... I'll go for that one!"

www.vitalcoaching.com

He must respect your personal space

When you live together, you are the owners of the space you live in.

You do this together.

Having pictures of his ex around the house is not the best way to validate your relationship.

Your house is dedicated to one thing: your partnership.

This means that your task is to preserve and protect your personal space.

If he wants to keep memories or old letters from past relationships, you can't stop him.

However, you can make sure that he keeps all that with his personal things.

You have the right to have some control over what happens in your personal space.

So, dare to express that power.

This is definitely okay as long as you are not trying to control his actions, beliefs or emotions.

If you have your own house and live separately, the same applies: ultimately you are the one who decides what happens in your home and what comes in or not.

Obsessive jealousy comes from a need to secure your life.

You know he is a window into your existence and you don't want to lose control.

This is why you tend to limit his freedom.

Now, the moment you gain back full control over your personal space, you gain back a very high level of security.

This is your right.

www.vitalcoaching.com

It is healthy to stay in charge of your personal environment.

If you live together, you share this authority.

You express this authority by taking decisions together, talking about boundaries and limits and using diplomacy when you discover an area of tension or conflict.

www.vitalcoaching.com

Have a constructive chat on relationship boundaries

One of the best ways to strengthen you couple is to find out EXACTLY what is ok and what is not in your relationship.

You often uncover that you both want the same.

Here are some ideas to start a conversation on boundaries:

- "How physical do you think it is ok for us to be with other people?"
- "Would it bother you if I was flirty with another guy in your presence?"
- "What exactly would bother you?"
- "Do you feel that the same boundary must apply to both of us or just one of us?"
- Etc.

This is a constructive conversation because there is no finger pointing or accusation.

You are not telling him what to do.

You ask for feed back.

You ask open ended questions.

You ask him to share.

This is why it gives him space to express what he feels.

The result? You design boundaries TOGETHER!

Because he designed the solution together with you, he embraces that choice rather than resenting it!

How often can you have a serious talk with him?

If you already had a constructive discussion a couple days ago, wait al least one to two weeks before you have another boundaries discussion.

Your couple can digest some "processing" but if you do it too frequently you don't give each other enough time and space to integrate new behaviors.

So, if you already had a serious chat recently, don't bring it up again even if something new comes up.

Instead, make a note of it and keep track of the points you would like to discuss when you have your next boundary chat.

You can journal on these issues.

Write down what works for you and what doesn't.

When a new element appears, keep track of it and don't bring it up straight away in a reactive way.

It is way better to wait for a few days until you can sit down again with him for a new in depth "boundary conversation".

www.vitalcoaching.com

He's doing it again! - Why doesn't he listen?

If you agreed on something and he crosses the line again, relax and give him some space and time to integrate this new behavior.

It often takes some repetition and revisiting the same issue a few times before a new behavior is really implemented.

Don't be too impatient with him. He's a human being!

Give him space for imperfections.

It's ok.

Next time he does something you disapprove of, repeat this mantra to yourself:

"He is not perfect and that's ok".

"I am not perfect either".

The long distance challenge

With long distance relationships, you need to take the same qualities of complicity and trust and multiply them by ten.

When you are at home and there is no way for you to check on your partner, it is only trust, power and inner confidence which can stop you from doubting about yourself and your relationship.

The place you "retreat" to is yourself.

You develop this extra power in you to strengthen your emotional foundation.

Suppose you feel unwanted jealousy waking up.

You are not confronted with a real threat.

Your mind is projecting pictures, images and visions.

Your mind is creating it, right?

These "betrayal dreams" are like spirits teasing you.

The way to protect your mind is to gain extra power.

Again, these obsessive emotional loops are not different from negative thinking.

They are self destructive loops which drain your energy.

They create doubts and fears in your mind.

Your imagination plays tricks on you.

Is it reality? Well, it could be...

Yes, you partner could be having an affair 2000 miles from where you are.

Suppose it is the case.

Suppose he is truly sleeping with another woman right now?

What would you do?

www.vitalcoaching.com

How would you shift your life and attitude?

To tell you the truth, yes! It can happen to any one any time.

It is possible.

The goal is to have a <u>constructive battle strategy</u> ready for that just in case it happens.

Doubts and insecurities are self destructive loops.

The best way to be prepared is to have a solid strategy in case it happens. This includes a solid material base.

You have your own financial resources, personal foundation and sources of power.

You maintain a reasonable level of independence and autonomy.

You can survive by yourself.

You have emergency funds you can use.

These are constructive prevention measures. They are a form of life insurance ready to use in case something happens.

You are in a couple situation but never forget about your own individual autonomy.

Before you "functioned" in a couple, you were an individual.

This individual integrity and autonomy is the place you would go back if something happened.

When you know how to do that, it gives you extra security.

You know you can survive anyway.

The result?

Your level of security increases immensely.

Why is that?

Because your life does not depend on your partner's actions any more.

www.vitalcoaching.com

This feeling of emotional and material autonomy gives you inner trust and security.

You play two roles in your love life:

- The first one is as an individual.
- The second one is as member of a couple.

The day you forget about your individual integrity, it makes you very vulnerable and dependent.

It stimulates more insecurity in you.

Your individual integrity is a power base.

Again, this is the true core of your individual.

Sometimes, you will invest in a relationship, but your individual autonomy never dies.

It gives you immense power to stay aware of that.

Does this means that you don't engage in your relationship?

Not at all!

You simply invest yourself in a different way.

Instead of abandoning yourself, you take smaller more measured steps.

When you get emotionally closer and more committed to your partner, you feel complicity building up.

If you suddenly feel insecure, jealous or possessive, it is the sign that you are loosing contact with your own individual base.

You become dependent, clingy and demanding.

This is not a good sign.

Step back slightly and find the right "emotional distance between" you and your partner.

Find the exact healthy level of commitment between the two of you.

www.vitalcoaching.com

A healthy level of commitment means that you feel no ache and no insecurity.

If you feel insecurity waking up, it can mean two things:

- You already give too much and expect from this relationship more than he does.
- The complicity and trust between the two of you needs to build up and you are working on it.

This is the art of finding an "emotional posture" which does not hurt.

If you stick your hand in a fire, you feel the heat and step back.

Creating power is the art of finding the right emotional investment towards your relationship: one which empowers you in a constructive way rather than consuming you in a self destructive flow of obsessive emotions.

www.vitalcoaching.com

How do you deal with jealousy in a long distance relationship?

Long distance means that you have all the challenges of a normal relationship + the distance.

The fact that you can't check what your boyfriend or husband does means that you need to multiply your level of trust.

The way to solve unwanted jealousy is the same as if you were living together. You train your "trust muscle" and reinforce respect and freedom.

With internet tools like webcam chat and email, distance is no longer what it used to be.

Every now and then, have a deep conversation to see if your relationship gives you both what you want.

If you notice any dissatisfaction, take action to make sure that your relationship stays exciting even with the distance.

How to keep your relationship exciting is a whole different topic.

The first step though is how to tame a jealousy response when it appears and turn it into trust.

www.vitalcoaching.com

Why supporting him financially makes you prone to jealousy

Yes! Taking financial responsibility for him can make you more prone to jealousy outbursts.

It opens a door!

It increases your expectations!

It makes you feel that you have the right to tell him what to do.

In other terms, it radically shifts the dynamics of how you relate to him.

What is the solution?

Does it mean that if you don't want to feel jealousy, you must not give him money?

Does it mean that if he wants to start his own business and you have the resources, you must not help him?

Well...

Ask yourself this question:

What is the deal?

What do you expect in return?

Would you still finance him if he wants to go partying with his female friends or go on dates with his ex?

Really! What is the deal?

Is it a gift or a loan?

What if you break up or he meets someone else?

Will you still help him financially?

How will this affect you emotionally?

www.vitalcoaching.com

Usually, having this financial link brings new challenges.

If you are both financially and materially independent, you manifest a higher level of freedom.

What is left between the two of you is really love and attraction!

These are the true binding forces!

Now, if the core binding force is a financial agreement you end up playing a very different game.

What will he say if you don't help him financially?

"No money? No boyfriend!"

Would this be his answer?

Or would it be:

"Money is not an issue between the two of us. I thank you for your honesty and I'll find another way of supporting myself. It changes nothing between you and me. I love you for who you are, not for whatever money or support you would have given me!"

How would your boyfriend respond?

Dare to ask yourself this question and face the facts, whatever they are.

So, what does this have to do with jealousy?

The money you give him is an investment.

You invest in him who is part of your life.

You usually expect something in return, whether it's conscious or unconscious.

Giving him money is not just a free gift.

The unspoken conditions are probably that you do expect some form of commitment on his side.

Because you give more (not just love), you expect more!

www.vitalcoaching.com

Now, he might not realize or even accept this.

Is he saying?

"Because you support me financially, it gives you the right to tell me what to do"

Of course not!

The unspoken contract is never discussed in detail! It stays very vague!

This is why supporting him financially can mean trouble for your relationship.

Because this agreement is unspoken and there is no clear "contract" you are left only with powers like jealousy and control to enforce it.

This is why giving him money can make you more prone to jealousy.

It is simply a natural instinctual response to this situation.

Like with any other jealousy triggers, increased awareness is already a big part of the solution.

You can avoid the trigger altogether or face it with greater awareness and new tools.

You have two choices:

- You can pull back and refuse to support him.

Or

- You can support him financially but discuss these unspoken conditions before you take the step.

Both directions can work.

If you are faced with this situation, trust your instincts and keep these ideas in mind when making your final choice.

If you still did not take a small tryout the step and observe how this impacts on your relationship.

If it impacts it negatively you can simply stop offering him support.

www.vitalcoaching.com

How datable is he?

Some guys simply don't want to be committed!

They like their freedom and won't make concessions on that, which is fine!

If you show up in their lives and try to make them be exclusive, you crash!

Your two plans don't match!

He has his agenda!

You have yours!

They don't match!

When you start dating a guy, you can easily identify if he is someone who will commit or not.

You will see warning signs:

- He does not return your calls!
- He lies!
- Talks a lot about exes and sexual adventures.
- He gets loads of female attention when you go out and forgets about you.
- He is young and openly says he wants to explore his sexuality.
- He is very flirty and is obviously on a hunt!
- Etc.

When you see these signs, you can easily reject or deny them.

You might think:

"He is confusing!"

"He gives me mixed signals!"

"I don't fully get him!"

When in fact, he is crystal clear!

Through his actions, he is telling you exactly what he wants.

The fact that you went on a couple of dates doesn't mean he wants to commit!

You assume he wants but it might not be his intention at all!

Maybe he even fools himself and say he wants exclusiveness while behaving like he's single!

He might say things like:

"We are so good together!"

"I love you!"

"I am so glad we met!

He might even get jealous and make a scene over you calling your ex!

This is the moment you need to be really smart as a woman!

Look at his actions! They speak louder than his words!

Does this mean you can't date him? Of course you can!

Simply lower your expectations and stop expecting full commitment.

We talk about a specific type of guys who enjoy their freedom.

He is not asking for change!

My guess is that probably half the guys you meet fit in that category.

You need to recognize them in the early stages.

Why?

Because if you don't you will easily feel unwanted jealousy triggered in you.

You feel jealous because you believe he is committed when in fact he is not!

www.vitalcoaching.com

This can confuse you.

That's the last thing you want.

Remember that if he is not committed to you, your jealousy is unjustified.

You can play with that emotion of course but there is no "territory" to defend.

Expressing jealousy and possessiveness will most likely mess up your connection and drive him away.

If he likes his freedom, he has probably been faced with similar situations before.

He's probably ready to step back at the slightest sign of possessiveness coming from you.

The only way to still date him is to respect his choices.

www.vitalcoaching.com

Part 6 - His exes, female friends and world

Tell him that I don't like him being in touch with ex?

First thing to check:

When did you have your last "boundaries" discussion with him?

If it's more than a couple weeks, it is possible to have a new open heart discussion about this.

If you want a chat, instead of saying: "When you interact with him, I don't like it and I think you should stop..."

Say:

"Let's chat about exes today... How close do you feel it is appropriate for them to be? For instance would you be ok with me exchanging text messages with my ex in the evening while you and I are together?"

"What do you feel is ok or not - What's your opinion? I am really interested in knowing what you think..."

You don't tell him what to do.

You bring it up and let him design a solution with you.

Keep this type of chat short and targeted.

Let him see that you are ok with whatever direction he wants to take.

However, he must know that if he chats with his ex you will connect with your exes too.

Will he be ok with that?

Another opportunity to practice your favorite mirror tactics ;)

www.vitalcoaching.com

He keeps pictures of his exes

His past relationships are part of his life. It is his past.

Having some memories of this past is okay as long as this does not keep you from evolving together.

If you don't want to see these pictures, ask him to keep them with his personal belongings. That's fair enough, right?

I mean, would he be pleased if you were hanging a picture of your ex on the living room's wall?

He can do what he wants with his belongings.

Let it go and don't be bothered. That's of course unless he leaves these pictures on the kitchen table.

Then, it is okay to tell him.

www.vitalcoaching.com

Your husband lies about an ex girlfriend

Imagine that your partner lies about interacting with an ex girlfriend.

You discover that he is lying to you.

What do you do?

Confront him?

Call her and tell her to stay away from your partner?

Let's check this:

Confronting him is usually the best way to go.

Now, if you accuse him of lying you need to have real proofs, not just vague feelings.

Proofs are records of his calls, a note from her or pictures of them together.

It is whatever tells you for sure that he is lying to you.

Now, when you confront him, you don't have to attack him or even be angry.

Take a special moment for the two of you.

Look at him in the eyes and say something like:

"What I am going to say will be challenging for both of us. The reason I bring this up is because I believe something is happening which destroys what we share."

After that, simply tell him:

"I know you have been speaking with your ex and lied to me about it. What do you think we should do about this?"

Of course he might fight back and accuse you of spying on him.

If he does, simply ask him:

"What do you suggest?"

That's it.

Use this situation as an opportunity to strengthen dialogue between the two of you.

The second option is to call his ex and ask her what she wants with him.

This will clarify the situation and help you decide for the best next strategy.

Remember that she might lie to you. So don't take her words as the ultimate truth.

Ask her if she realizes that he has been lying to you.

Tell her as well that right now, this has the power to destroy your relationship.

In this situation, there are two directions the situation can evolve.

She might understand, feel complicity with you and decide to pull back or she might fight back because she wants him.

If she fights back, you need to shift gears and go to battle mode.

Ultimately it will definitely be your partner's final choice. If he has two options, it is really up to him to decide what he wants.

However, you can of course rebuild attraction and strengthen complicity with him.

This is a vast topic in itself.

I cover it in depth in the "How to empower your relationship" book available on vitalcoaching.com

Can you call his ex? Is this okay?

Let's check the previous example a bit deeper.

When he lies to you about an ex or another girl he is seeing, your relationship is under attack.

It is coming from a very specific source.

This is a situation where jealousy is 100% justified.

It is okay to do whatever it takes to preserve your relationship.

Use whatever power is given to you to fight back!

It is okay to call her or send her an email.

A word from you and she might pull back.

She will feel complicity with you especially if you have children for instance or if she is simply a kind and smart person.

You can contact her and ask her to step back.

Don't beg!

Don't apologize!

Be direct and firm.

It is your relationship!

You are given the right to protect it.

Now is the time to use your power.

Dare to express it.

Use your fighting power and clear the space.

For him, having contact with an ex partner is okay.

<u>Lying to you is not!</u>

Other women must know that you are there and will defend your territory.

Dare!

You'll feel relieved and immensely empowered when you do.

Stand behind your actions and if your partner questions your move, tell him exactly why you did it.

www.vitalcoaching.com

Insecure about your partner's past experiences

If you are insecure about your partner's past experiences?

Please don't be!

The answer to this challenge is simple: you want extra power.

You compare yourself to your partner.

There is a misbalance.

He is with you right now.

It is with you he decides to be.

His past is his.

You can't change it and you won't.

You need to convince yourself of this right now.

Right now, you are the special person he decides to be with.

Delete your insecurity and tap into this extra strength inside yourself.

It is you he values.

It is with you he decides to be.

Trust his love and give this love back to him.

His love is a gift for you.

There is nothing you can do about his past.

The only thing you can do is shift the way you stand in this.

When you embrace someone, you embrace everything about that person.

You can't reject half of it.

www.vitalcoaching.com

You need to accept the person you love <u>as a whole</u>.

It is complete.

What he gives you right now is the result of his past experiences as well.

Accept it as a gift.

Embrace his full being.

www.vitalcoaching.com

Is it okay for him to have a female friend?

The answer is yes!

The number one reason for break ups is too much control within the relationship.

If your couple is too constricting, sooner or later you either break up or become very unhappy.

Encourage mutual freedom in your couple.

The real base of your relationship is not mutual control; it is mutual trust and love.

When you commit to your partner, you usually decide to be sexually exclusive.

This is the real boundary.

Boundaries are designed consciously, together.

You identify exactly what works for both of you.

For instance, some couples decide to have an open relationship because they like the freedom.

What is important is to design these boundaries together.

Dialogue! Diplomacy!

I encourage you to relax about his female friends and realize this simple fact:

It is still with you he decides to be.

It is with you he shares his life.

It is with you he is intimate.

So, it's simple!

Drop it and trust him!

www.vitalcoaching.com

Trying to control his social life is a no-win situation.

Allow other women to validate him.

It says that he chooses for you even though he has other options.

That's a fantastic way to see his interactions with other women.

www.vitalcoaching.com

How to deal with him having female friends

Is it okay for your partner to have male friends? Sure it is.

It validates him and refreshes your relationship.

You have two options:

- Be controlling demanding and freaking out.

Or

- Letting it go and even enjoying it

The real alternative is for you to have male friends as well.

Again, open communication is what works best.

Talk about it with your partner and find out about your real boundaries.

The rules are the same for both.

If he can't take it, then obviously there is no reason for you to take it either.

Limiting each other's space kills the relationship.

Staying in touch with good friends and having time off out of the relationship is healthy.

It is of course a slight challenge and a stretch of your comfort zone but it is worth it.

On the long term everyone benefits from it.

Remember, it is still with you he decides to be.

You stay number one.

www.vitalcoaching.com

What to do when you see him chat with another woman

Imagine you are at a party and you see him having a chat with a woman.

Simple, stop watching and take action.

If he is focused on someone else, the best response is for you to focus on someone else as well.

Don't wait for him to come back.

Go and engage a conversation with another man as well.

Your partner can only give you so much validation.

What gives you extra power is validation from other men as well.

Connect, exchange and open up.

The best way to overcome obsessive jealousy is to gain extra power and satisfaction.

If you don't feel too open, challenge yourself and go for it.

Don't isolate yourself.

Be socially outgoing!

Yes! It's okay to chat with another man.

Don't feel guilty about it.

You betray nobody by connecting with another guy.

Connecting is a natural human need.

As you get validation from other men, this boosts your self esteem and empowers you.

If you believe that no other male values you as a woman, this makes you very clingy and dependent

www.vitalcoaching.com

Give other men the opportunity to share a moment with you.

Discuss your insecurities if he chats with other girls?

Well, the question is: Do you even want to discuss it?

Did he cheat?

Did he betray you?

Did he do something wrong?

Or do you simply feel insecure?

I mean, is this issue in his hands or in your hands?

Is he your therapist or your lover?

Guys tend to get tired of having to reassure their partner endlessly.

It's exhausting to feel that no matter how hard you try, your partner still believes you are going to cheat on her.

So, the solution is to get things straight once and for all:

What are your relationship boundaries?

Are you committed to each other?

What is ok and what is not?

Once these are solved, don't bring up insecurities over and over again.

www.vitalcoaching.com

He's got female friends but I have no male friends

No need to develop deep friendships.

Being open to connect with men is enough.

- Flirt a bit.
- Chat with a guy you just met.
- Activate your social power when attending an event.
- Etc.

Once you realize that other men like you too, your level of power and confidence is REALLY boosted.

When you rely only on your partner for validation, this makes you very dependent on him.

If he is all you have, he having a simple chat with another woman will make you insecure.

Now, if for instance you are open to connect on Facebook with an old male friend who just found you, the balance is shifted instantly!

Let's get this right, ok?

The goal here is not to make him jealous. The goal is to have other sources of social validation in your life, not just your partner.

That's the key!

www.vitalcoaching.com

I react when he flirts with this girl at work

You react when you see a colleague flirt with him?

There is nothing wrong with you.

Your reaction is healthy and natural.

You react that way because you are not used to it.

You might be shocked to hear your partner flirt with another girl.

When you are new in a relationship, you search to find the right boundaries and a way to stand in situations like these.

Is it okay to flirt with someone else or not?

Should your partner shut down and stop talking to other girls at all?

Is it okay to flirt as long as you know he stays faithful to you?

Is it okay to flirt but you don't want to see it or know about it?

You want to find out exactly what is okay and what is not.

These are called relationship boundaries.

Light flirt is usually okay, right?

He kissing someone else is usually not.

There is some form of natural balance which feels good for both of you.

These limits are very precise.

You want to define these limits together.

Talk about it with your partner and find out the exact limits which is okay for both of you.

www.vitalcoaching.com

For instance, if he thinks these light flirts at work are okay, he needs to be comfortable as well if the situation is reversed and you are the one flirting with a man.

The idea is to strengthen trust and complicity without limiting too much each other's space.

Think long term:

What are the limits which feel good and healthy on the long term and give you both enough space and freedom without threatening the couple's stability?

Too much control in the relationship kills the magic.

This is why these limits are very subtle to establish.

One step too far and you blow it off and limit your partner.

One step behind and you feel awkward and insecure.

Talk openly with your partner and find the right limits for both of you.

www.vitalcoaching.com

Jealous of the women he works with

Is your partner a flirt?

Is he surrounded by a couple of attractive colleagues?

The question is:

What can you do about it?

Maybe you too take some lessons with an attractive fitness trainer.

Maybe you have a secret crush on one of your colleagues.

These situations happen in life.

Can you stop them from happening? No. It is simple.

You need to keep on living.

Light flirts are okay as long as you don't act on them.

It is okay for your partner to have contact with other women, even if they are handsome and very attractive.

The truth is that he is with you.

It is with you he decides to be.

Spending time with others is healthy. It is part of life to work with others.

This won't change.

What you can change is the way you respond to it.

Communicate openly with your partner. There is no taboo!

The moment you can share and tease each other with it, you bring this whole issue to something very light and even fun.

Infidelity is an act. It is not a thought. It is not a fantasy.

www.vitalcoaching.com

It is okay to dream, to look and to enjoy someone's company.

This is not a crime.

It is not infidelity.

It is natural and healthy to get validation from other people.

It is okay to lightly flirt with someone.

If your relationship's boundaries are too tight, you limit yourself and constrict the relationship.

You simply asphyxiate it!

The solution is to establish a higher level of trust.

Talk about it with your partner. Be light and open about it.

Accept these situations as part of life.

Remember: It is still with you he decides to be.

If you are in a committed relationship, there is a moral agreement between the two of you. Looking at another woman does not break this moral agreement.

Give each other some space. It is healthy and truly beneficial for the relationship.

Give him the gift of your trust.

If you see him chatting with another woman, you can as well express a positive form of jealousy.

It is okay to claim your partner and show the world you two are together.

Do this if he is comfortable with it: go and kiss him front of other women and send a clear message that he is not available.

This is a healthy type of action and is a "couple statement".

It is an affirmation of your mutual love.

Can you see how it works?

www.vitalcoaching.com

The key is always trust and complicity.

He goes for after work drinks with his female colleagues

Do the same!

The moment you have your own set of male admirers, believe me, the whole power balance in your relationship shifts.

The reason you feel threatened by this is because you feel left out.

Many guys hate their job and have zero opportunities for interesting social interaction within the work environment!

If he's having the time of his life, you might feel that it's not fair, right?

Boost your social connections and make sure that amongst them you have a couple of very attractive males.

This is really the ultimate strategy in this situation.

Don't wait at home for him to come back and unload the details of his latest discussions with his female admirers.

Instead take proactive steps and start connecting with other men fearlessly.

No shame! No guilt!

Remember that the key boundary in your relationship is probably: "No intimacy with someone else".

Having a chat with a male friend is NOT cheating.

It is chatting!

Chatting IS ok!

Never feel guilty for connecting with a man, no matter how attractive he is.

This is the type of action that can actually trigger a whole chain reaction of interesting conversations with your partner.

www.vitalcoaching.com

For instance, if he hears about it and starts feeling slightly insecure or challenges you about it, here is what you can say:

YOU - "So, you think that I should not speak with other men than you???"

HIM - "Well... He is obviously into you otherwise he would never have given you his number..."

YOU - "So, you believe that you meeting your female colleagues after work is different?

HIM - "Absolutely! They are just friends..."

YOU - "So, if I was working with a VERY attractive male colleague and I was going with him for drinks after work, you would be ok with that?"

HIM - "Well... I would need to be sure that you won't cheat on me!!! When a guy spends time with a woman there is ALWAYS potential for something more!"

YOU - "So, when you have a chat with a female colleague, there is always potential for more???"

GOT YOU!

You see? Right there, you just nailed it!

That's called mirroring the situation back to him.

You just made him understand EXACTLY how it feels to be in your shoes when he is at a bar having a drink with colleagues.

Now, you are not saying that he has to stop.

You are saying that:

- A few words of reassurance in your direction might help.
- He needs to understand the exact boundary between what is ok and what is not.
- If he does it, he needs to be able to take it from you as well.

www.vitalcoaching.com

- 185 -

My point is that the moment you decide to do the same, it forces him to look at his own patterns + come up with relationship boundaries that work well for both of you.

If you simply walk to him with a needy voice and ask him who these girls are, you will feel totally powerless in this conversation.

He will put you down and smother you with an "Oh... They are just friends... Do you feel threatened by that??"

You don't have to beg!

Take the step and simply practice this mirror strategy!

Meet your own set of male friends and observe carefully what happens next...

www.vitalcoaching.com

He prefers chatting with his buddies

Guys can share lots of stuff he won't ever share with you.

What he gets from you might be totally different than what he gets from his buddies.

That's ok, right?

It is with you he is engaged in a romantic relationship.

Now, if you feel you lack emotional intimacy with him, that's a connection you can consciously build up.

If you want him to open up to you more, he needs to feel emotionally secure with you.

It is hard for him to trust you if your conversations evolve a lot around problems and challenging issues.

He needs to be able to relax when he has a conversation with you.

What does that mean?

- You don't attack him when he shares something.
- You ask him follow up questions like "Can you tell me more?".
- You listen and acknowledge what he says.
- Etc.

Men love sharing once they realize you enjoy his sharing.

Asking follow up questions is a coaching technique that you can ad to your conversation skills.

Here are more examples:

- "Tell me more about that..."
- "If I get you right, you are saying that..."
- "So, what would you do if..."

These are all invitations to share.

Back to his mates, how should you react?

www.vitalcoaching.com

- Let him know that you are happy for him having these friends.
- Be ok when he has a night out with them.
- Be friendly with these guys when they come for a visit.

You REALLY don't need to compete with them.

Having them ads value to his life and expands your network as a couple.

www.vitalcoaching.com

I am not invited to the party

You are dating this guy and he goes to a party to which you are not invited.

It might be a male only event, work related or school reunion type.

This can happen, right?

The first question to ask yourself is:

Is this justified?

Am I not invited because he's got an issue with seeing me there?

Or is this simply an external rule he can't change?

In some cases he can actually get you there but prefers not to, for some reason.

He might resist introducing you to some old friends or family members.

If he has got an issue with bringing you to that event, and you would like to go, you need of course to sit down with him and talk about his resistance.

After that, you might be able to remove his fears or doubts and help him change his decision.

If the final decision of inviting your or not is out of his hands, you need to simply accept it and make the best of it.

Plan something with a friend for that evening or have a relaxing evening for yourself.

www.vitalcoaching.com

He looks at porn

Porn is similar to any other form of addictive behaviors.

It can be compared to alcohol, substance abuse or gambling behaviors.

Some small doses of these behaviors can be okay.

Even if you don't like them, you can learn to tolerate and accept them.

Now if it comes to the point where it is really disturbing your relationship and making you miserable, here are three directions this situation can take:

If your partner is smart and open, he will be okay with shifting his porn oriented behaviors.

This is a real opportunity to grow together as a couple.

Talk about it and if he is open for it, educate him!

Refer to the MP3 audios on "how to educate your partner" in your online program.

What if he refuses to change or talk about it?

Of course, you can learn to accept this.

What if you can't?

What if this drives you mad and you can't stand his behavior?

Well, porn can be a deal breaker for your relationship.

Couples do break up over this issue.

Imagine that you live with someone who needs to be high every Saturday night and you can't stand it.

Or take the situation where your partner's spending behaviors bring your couple to financial bankruptcy.

www.vitalcoaching.com

All these situations have something in common: you fundamentally disagree on key life style choices.

Ask yourself:

"How much longer do I want to tolerate this behavior?"

"Can I see myself with him 5 years from now if he does not change?"

"What are the chances of him changing his attitude?"

A third option is to explore new aspects of your sexuality together.

This could reorient his desire and wake up new passion dimensions in the core of your couple.

This is a vast topic.

Check the "Sex" section on vitalcoaching.com for more on this.

His work always comes first!

Here are some ideas

He can work as much as he wants!

That's his time!

That's his career!

He is free!

This is the general idea.

Trying to limit him or force him to spend time with you will achieve the exact opposite to what you want.

What you can do is openly invite him for things which are fun and let him make his own choices.

You can say things like:

"We'll be going out with Paul, his girlfriend and two other buddies to this new club... I heard it is pretty fantastic! I know you often need to stay late at work on Friday so, you are of course totally free to choose if you want to join us or not..."

You see, the moment you try to force him, it triggers a defense response in him.

If you offer him an open invitation it becomes his choice to do what he wants with it.

If he is too busy with work, don't stay at home waiting for him.

Develop your own set of activities that don't depend on him.

Make new friends, go out and respond to invitations.

You don't need to share everything.

www.vitalcoaching.com

He systematically chooses for his kids

If you are dating a single father, this will happen and it is VERY natural!

His kids are his life.

They will always come first!

They need his protection and love.

So, be prepared!

Does this mean that such relationship can't work?

Of course not!

You still have lots of possibilities to connect.

Take another example:

If you have your own business for instance and this takes lots of your time, you won't drop everything just because he wants you to, right?

This is your life!

His kids are his and they were a family before you met him.

You don't need to compete with them for attention.

If you feel he doesn't give you enough time, check with him.

He might be open to create more.

You do that without pressure.

Say something like: "I suddenly had this idea of taking off for a week end together – these friends offered me to use their holiday house – Is this something you would like?"

This is an open invitation and he is free to respond to it or not.

www.vitalcoaching.com

Part 7 - Worried he will cheat? – Spying on him?

Is there a way to make sure that he never cheats on you?

Here is what you can do to protect your couple.

- Make sure that he gets his needs met in your relationship.
- You are at your best and attractive!
- You share and communicate openly in your couple.
- You keep your sex life exciting.
- He gets the attention he needs from you.
- You take time to be romantic, passionate and nurture your love life.
- You make plans for the future.
- You keep on evolving together.
- You stay in good shape and take good care of yourself, your social life and career.
- Etc.

It's all about "Attraction"!

The more he is attracted to you, the less he will need to look somewhere else.

You stay attractive by expressing your power and confidence.

You keep your life interesting and moving forward!

Don't put him on a leash!

Here is what would send him away:

- Trying to control his activities and being over jealous and possessive.
- Asking him for endless emotional support.
- Expressing your insecurities to him and hoping he will solve them for you.
- Getting stacked in your life and stopping taking risks.
- Being enslaved by an addiction or self destructive behavior.

www.vitalcoaching.com

- Focusing your life too much on comfort and not enough on excitement.
- Failing to keep your sex life exciting!
- Etc!

There is much more of course.

If the relationship is exciting, he has no reason to look somewhere else.

Now a big mistake you might make is to believe that security and comfort are the most important factors.

You get comfort with a nice house, wealth and emotional security.

These count only for 1/3 in the relationship's equation.

Thrill, excitement and fresh perspectives take as much space in his mind.

Creating together an exciting and passionate sex life is the best way to keep him.

www.vitalcoaching.com

Afraid that your partner is cheating on you?

What makes you believe he is?

Picture it realistically.

How is this happening?

When?

What are your proofs?

After that, confront your suspicions with real facts.

If he says he is at work and you believe he is not, check it out.

Call him or drive there.

Test it!

Test your suspicions and find real answers to the questions you ask yourself.

If you find answers and they prove you wrong, listen!

Don't deny them!

These are the real facts you were looking for.

My father cheated on my mother – Now I can't trust men!

Trust is like a bridge you walk on.

In the beginning, you are not sure if it will stand strongly.

It is a bridge made of love and respect.

These are values you learn to strengthen in yourself.

They are key pillars and attitudes you learn to reinforce in your being.

If your instinctual reaction is to be afraid of trusting because you had negative experiences in the past, the goal is to rebuild trust and regain confidence when relating to men and people in general.

How do you do that?

First, don't forget about the past experience.

Any experience is a learning one.

It is true, sometimes, men do cheat.

Sometimes, people will betray you.

If you try to simply pretend it does not exist, you'll probably get hurt again.

The goal is to develop skills to evolve in the territory of relationships with greater awareness and ability to respond to challenges.

You need to expand your awareness and think beyond black and white.

Humans are not good or bad. They have two sides to them.

The goal is to be able to relate harmoniously and constructively to the positive aspects and protect yourself against what could hurt you.

It would be a mistake to simply trust blindly anyone any time.

www.vitalcoaching.com

You want to stay awake and develop your loving and fighting skills simultaneously.

There is no need to be naive or hide yourself in some form of utopist tower.

The art of trusting is the art of staying awake.

You listen to warning signs.

You are realistic about what a man is or is not.

The moment you are given real reasons to trust, you go with it and increase the level of complicity with a man who obviously cares for you.

When you have been hurt in the past (indirectly, because in fact it happened to your mother), you create patterns which tends to attract back similar situations until this is truly solved.

The goal is to find out what to do in such situations.

You can go back to this situation in the past and analyze what happened exactly.

If this situation was happening again, what would you do?

How would you react to it?

The goal is to "face these events" again and realize that you would not go for passivity.

In fact you would wake up new fighting skills.

Cheating is a form of betrayal and if you simply tolerate it, it will happen again until you wake up and fight it in your own unique way.

How do you fight it?

First, you wake up your jealousy weapons.

This is the moment jealousy is a healthy response to a threat.

You see, jealousy is often see as a purely negative reaction.

In fact this is far from true.

www.vitalcoaching.com

- 199 -

Jealousy can be a positive psychic weapon you use to defend your territory.

If a woman comes anywhere near your relationship, it is okay to express your power and send a clear signal.

This is the first step: mastering your "jealousy weapon".

If a man you are with already cheated, you have to wake your next set of "fighting" skills.

If you feel emotionally abused in this situation and an open relationship was never an option, it is time to go to your partner and confront him.

Most women would simply leave their partner in such situation.

The skills you want to develop are your ability to choose for break up rather than abusive relationship situation.

In a way, these fighting skills are your ability to defend your own well being.

You see cheating as betrayal and you have a clear limit and boundary you don't want any man to cross.

In your situation, this means that you need to develop new relationship "weapons". The first step is to dare to express your jealousy weapon when needed.

The second step is to have a set of strategies ready in case cheating happens.

You can see these strategies as a form of "life insurance". You know that if a man cheats, you have a set of emergency emotional and material resources you can tap into any time.

Basically, this means having the power to walk away from a relationship which is not fulfilling for you.

This is the skill that you mother missed, right?

Maybe, the time or cultural set up did not allow her to take that step.

www.vitalcoaching.com

Maybe she did not find the power to walk away or was simply worried about what would happen to her or her children.

Now, times have changed. The situation you are in today gives you the right and power to walk away from a relationship which is abusive in any way.

The moment you realize you have that power and are ready to use it if needed, you break a cycle.

You break a family pattern and set up a new course for your life and for those around you.

The moment you break a "family" pattern and decide once and for all that staying in an abusive relationship situation is not okay, you set up a new course in your life.

Basically, you free yourself from something your mother indirectly taught you.

I know this is challenging, but what you do is simply telling your mother and father: "this situation was not okay!"

"I know exactly what I would do if this situation was arising in my life."

"I know it would be a battle but I know I would win this battle"

"I would never let a man treat me like that"

Maybe one day you will need to use these weapons.

Maybe, you will meet a caring man who will never betray you in any way.

What matters is that you have all tools and resources you need, just in case.

Dare to express your full power!

www.vitalcoaching.com

He cheated before! - I am worried he will cheat again!

If he cheated before your jealousy is justified.

Something is definitely unsolved!

If your partner cheated you need to heal the open wounds and hurt created by this experience.

You do that through dialogue and rebuilding complicity.

If he can't guarantee you that he won't cheat again, you have to shift the way your attitude and protect yourself.

You can either decide to stay together or leave him

How can you protect yourself without leaving him?

You take some emotional distance and gain more independence from him.

You gain back your financial, material and social freedom.

This means that you have your own source of income, a nice circle of friends, and maybe even your own place.

If he can't guarantee to be faithful, you need a solid back up plan in case he cheats again.

Another way to go is to reaffirm your own limits and be firm:

"If you cheat again, our relationship is over! Got that?"

A last option is to create an open relationship.

This means that you are no longer sexually exclusive in your couple and you are both free to have other lovers.

This last option is quite a challenge and maybe only 5% of couples are open for it.

www.vitalcoaching.com

If he cheated before

Obviously, cheating kills mutual trust.

If you partner cheated but honestly regrets his actions asks for forgiveness, there is a chance to rebuilt trust and a strong couple.

This experience can even empower your relationship and create a refreshed connection between you and him.

You realize how much you care for each other.

If you realize that he is not 100% committed to you and that cheating could happen again, you are trying to protect a very unstable territory.

It takes two strong pillars to preserve the relationship's space.

You can't do that alone.

He is not 100% committed?

Fine! You can't force him!

The solution?

Step back as well.

Flirt with other men.

If he reacts, ask him if he is 100% committed to you and if he could be running away with another woman any time soon.

Can you see the dynamics?

Don't give your life to someone who does not give it back to you.

If he is uncommitted and you are committed, it drains you.

It creates an emotional tension in your system. It is like a need or desire you can't fulfill.

You wait for him to take steps.

The solution?

www.vitalcoaching.com

Step back as well and recover part of what you invested in him.

Take your freedom back.

You need extra power and determination to do this!

He wants to keep his freedom?

Fine! Take your freedom back too!

Should you check on him?

Suppose you have doubts.

You have the feeling he is not telling the truth.

Should you take action and for instance check his emails or follow him after work?

Is it okay to spy on your partner?

The answer is yes.

But you need to be very careful with what you do and why you do it.

95% of obsessive jealousy situations are unfounded.

In fact, jealousy is often delusional.

You imagine things that don't exist.

You interpret signs in extreme ways.

Basically, you distort reality.

If you have doubts, find out the truth.

Here are some very specific limits you must respect.

Talk to him first!

Before you spy on your partner or invade his privacy, talk to him and ask him direct questions.

If you think he is lying, I encourage you to take steps and check the facts.

Be very careful with how you interpret facts.

Finding a woman's phone number in his agenda is not a proof of cheating!

It is simply a proof that he is in contact with another woman.

This is not cheating, yet!

www.vitalcoaching.com

Get ALL the facts before making any assumptions!

Spying is a step that must be taken only as a last resort.

If your intention is to set up hidden cameras in your partner's car for instance (just to be sure), this obviously crosses the line.

This is not a game. It is a last resort battle strategy aimed at defending your life and relationship.

It is better to verify doubts or feelings with real facts rather than letting them build up in your mind.

If after spying you realize it was all an illusion, remember this next time you have these same cheating doubts waking up again.

Get the answers and learn from it!

www.vitalcoaching.com

Stop spying on him!

Some ways of spying are quite innocent.

Let's call this "level 1" spying.

In fact it is not even called spying.

It is called being curious.

In involves simple elements like recognizing the hand writing on the envelope of a letter he just received.

Another time, you might over hear a phone conversation he has with an ex simply because you happen to be there.

It happens because you are confronted with it. You were not really looking for it.

When you ask him where he has been, or what he did, it can be along the same line. This is sneakier and can be more invasive though.

You will say things like:

"I was worried about you!"

When in fact you were wondering with who he was and why he was not home at 6 as usual.

This attitude can become invasive if it is systematic.

The next level of spying (level 2) is when you actively take action to check what he's up to.

This involves checking his profile on a dating site to see if he has been active on it lately.

It is still non invasive because you don't betray his privacy. His profile is online for everyone to see.

In the next stage (level 3), you definitely cross the line:

- You check his cell phone records.
- You check his text messages.

www.vitalcoaching.com

- You enter his email account.
- You read his personal mail.
- You search his belongings looking for clues,
- Etc.

This one is a big No-No unless you have very good reasons to believe he is cheating on you.

It is an invasion of his privacy!

Realize that when you take that step, it could be a deal breaker for your relationship if he finds out about it.

There is one more level after that (level 4) which is following him, using detective tactics on him or hiring someone to do that!

The exact definition or model of these spying levels is not that important. I just made them up to make you realize that not all spying is the same.

You might easily indulge in a level 1 "spying-curiosity".

You ask general questions about his activities.

You are exposed to his life and know about some of his social connections.

That's okay.

If you took any other step (level 2-4) or you aggressively ask him invasive questions, you start expressing unwanted jealousy, right?

You want to get rid of that.

If you went to level 3 one time, thought he was cheating and found nothing, listen to this sign!

Forgive yourself and go back to the "I trust you" pattern.

The best way to stop spying on him is to consciously drop it.

When you are tempted, you sit down, wait for a minute and repeat to yourself:

"I am here to protect your freedom, not to limit you."

www.vitalcoaching.com

Depending on the intensity of your tendency to spy on him, it can easily take a month of focus to shift that behavior.

Even if you fall back, listen to the signs and what you found.

If he is not cheating, see it as a learning experience and use it to shift your behavior in the future.

If you found nothing, this usually means that your suspicions were ungrounded.

Spying on him is just another expression of your jealousy or insecurity. It is another way of expressing it.

Sometimes, you can express it verbally, other times you express it via this type of spying behaviors.

Ask yourself these questions:

What are the level, intensity and frequency of your spying/curiosity?

Does it bother either you or him?

This will tell you exactly how urgent it is for you to do something about it.

www.vitalcoaching.com

Should you tell him that you have been spying on him?

No, don't tell him!

Unless you found something and want to confront him.

It is not necessary!

Forgive yourself, realize that your suspicions were ungrounded and that you can in fact trust him.

When you spy on him, you take a risk!

If you feel guilty, live with your actions and forgive yourself.

Consider that you did what was right at that time.

It was your best shot at defending your relationship and showing that you cared.

Learn from that experience and discover exactly why you will not do it again:

- You realized that your fears were delusional.
- You prefer trusting him.
- You did change and mature emotionally.
- You were vulnerable and found yourself back.
- Etc.

If your couple is strong and you know that telling him would not be an issue, it is okay to open up of course.

However, many men can't tolerate this type of behavior and would be extremely offended if they found out!

It could destroy the trust he has in you!

If your priority is to protect your relationship, act accordingly and don't tell him anything he can't take.

If you think it was a mistake, it was yours, not his!

Deal with it!

www.vitalcoaching.com

Should you confront him if you know he is lying?

Yes! Definitely yes!

However you need to do it right.

First, you need proof that he is lying.

Maybe you spied on him and checked his email or cell phone.

This means that you have real proof, not just feelings.

If all you have are vague feelings, you can't confront him!

It won't work!

Once you have gathered solid proofs, realize as well that YOU spied on him!

He will accuse you of not trusting him.

The next step is to choose the right timing and attitude.

You don't want to point your finger at him and tell him how bad he is.

You want to sit down and have an open chat about what is going in your relationship.

That's if you still care and that you still want him.

If it is the case, the goal is to empower your relationship, not to find someone to blame.

Say something like:

"I face a challenge with our relationship and I need your help to solve this dilemma. When is a good time to talk about this?"

When you meet, you can be direct and say something like:

- What I am about to share with you is quite challenging.
- So be prepared...

www.vitalcoaching.com

- Please, let me speak for 5 min and don't interrupt me.
- You will have space to reflect on this when I am done.
- Some days ago, I felt something was wrong...
- I noticed...
- I decided to check this and followed you...
- I discovered that...

If he accuses you of spying on him, you can say:

"Yes! We both did something which betrays the trust in our relationship. We are both guilty. Now, what are we going to do about it? What do you suggest we do now?"

If he says:

"First, I need you to promise me that you won't spy on me again..."

You can say:

"If I have serious reasons to believe that you are cheating on me or lying to me, I will use any tool I can to find out the truth."

"Now, my turn! You cheated on me. How do you feel about what happened?"

You can decide after his sharing if you want to give your relationship a chance or if it's over.

www.vitalcoaching.com

Part 8 – From insecurity to total trust

Behind unwanted jealousy there is always a need to secure your life.

The way to develop a deeper sense of security in your existence is by empowering your life and your relationship.

Imagine your life and relationship as a territory.

You feel insecure the moment you feel vulnerable.

Why can you feel vulnerable?

Because you miss power.

In the next few pages, we will analyze key strategies to empower your life _and_ your relationship.

What is insecurity?

Insecurity is lack of power.

It is a gap in your emotional foundation.

Your mind is a territory.

When you feel insecure, you feel threatened.

It can be anything:

- Lack of material security
- Fear of other's judgment
- Anguish
- Fear of loosing your partner's love
- Lack of assertiveness and confidence
- Self esteem gap
- Fear of someone else's anger
- Insecurity with your body
- Etc.

The single solution to all these challenges is extra power.

Power is what gives you emotional stability.

When you feel insecure, your mind is invaded by negative emotions.

Jealousy is only the reflection of one form of insecurity.

However, power building strategies are effective with any form of insecurity.

When your mind is empowered and vital, you are not touched by irrational fears.

You feel empowered and see "attacks" simply bouncing on the surface of your mind.

When you strengthen your emotional foundation, you are safe.

50% of the insecurity challenge consists in accepting the idea of power.

www.vitalcoaching.com

<u>You have power in you</u>.

Sometimes, you forget to use it because a part of you rejects it.

You might focus on love only, pure harmony and reject the idea of battle, challenges and fight.

- **First step**

  <u>Get used to the idea of power in you</u>. When you take this step, you make yourself <u>conductive to power</u> rather than resistant to it.

- **Second step**

  <u>Use your will power</u> to get what you want. Stop being passive or receptive and create the life you want. <u>Determination makes a difference</u>. Be assertive, direct and head for your target.

- **Third step**

  <u>Develop effective strategies</u>. Once you wake up power and use determination, all you need is <u>skills and strategies</u>. A strategy is a mind set. This is what gives you victory.

The result is extra power.

This is the <u>ultimate solution to all your insecurities</u>.

When you develop extra power, you give yourself the tools to succeed.

How to shift your level of power

Emotional pain is a lack of life force and energy.

Jealousy is your way of calling for attention and help.

If you simply expect to be "emotionally fed", you can wait for a long time.

There is a gap.

It is an emotional gap. There is a gap because you don't receive what you want or expect.

You put too much stress on your partner and relationship.

The way to overcome jealousy is not to ask your partner to solve your insecurities; it is to wake up your personal power.

There is a source of power you are not using.

Why don't you use it?

Because you tend to forget it is in you.

Sometimes you tend to delegate your power to your partner.

If you want to stop the "pain", you need to wake up your individual power and connect with what happens beyond the couple's cell.

This can be your own career path, friends, body, etc.

Step beyond your comfort zone

Challenge yourself

Wake up your conquering power

Your couple's space is comfortable.

It is protected and preserved.

This is why you need extra conquering power to open up beyond the limits of the relationship.

www.vitalcoaching.com

The moment, you do, <u>it gives you confidence</u>.

Invest in goals you can relate to. When you take steps, you use your conquering power and wake up a new set of resources. You change gear and go from hesitation to definite action. This gives you a boost of energy and confidence.

Insecurity has to do with isolation. Jealousy happens because you don't get your needs met. Irrational insecurity often goes beyond what your partner can do for you.

<u>This is about you!</u>

It is about the way you relate to others, to the city you live in, to the planet, to your own destiny line.

<u>Wake up your power!</u>

This is the key to get rid of insecurity.

How to manifest security in your life

You want to expand the level of security in your life. You want to feel strong and secure.

Let's focus on that okay?

Ask yourself these simple questions concerning your inner feeling of security:

- **Where or how do you find security in life?**

- **Who or what can give it to you?**

- **What are elements in your existence which make you feel immensely secure?**

- **When you walk on the "bridge of trust" is there a way to secure your steps?**

- **Is there an infinite source of security you can tap into right now?**

Take a few minutes to find answers to these questions and write them down.

Find out exactly what security means for you and where you can find it.

www.vitalcoaching.com

Dissatisfaction and frustration

Sometimes, jealousy rises from frustration and life dissatisfaction.

Frustration is simply an inability to express yourself.

Suppose you have a good friend. She just got promoted at her work.

You on the other hand, are still waiting for a raise and you are frustrated about your situation.

When she tells you the good news ("Guess what happened to me today…"), you can feel jealous from her success.

This jealousy is the expression of your own frustration, right?

What goes on in your mind could sound like: "Jee! How come this did not happen to me?"

This jealous reaction does not help you reach your goals.

It is simply a competitive reaction.

It is a form of aggressive reaction like anger or hatred.

This can happen a lot within friendships or a social circle.

Are these little jealousies productive? Not really.

In fact, it might mess up your friendships and isolate you.

Are there alternatives?

Yes!

Focus on creating win-win attitudes and daring to put jealousy aside to empower those around you.

If something good happens to them and you are on the edge of reacting out of your own frustration, try putting your jealousy on hold and use your fighting fire to celebrate their success.

www.vitalcoaching.com

Jealousy – How to deal with it – For women

The idea is not to suppress your jealousy. The idea is to use your conquering fire in a different way: create win-wins and synergy with those around you.

Empower their successes and they will usually empower yours in return.

Waking up your own qualities of power, joy, love and pleasure is the real alternative.

Frustration is an emotional reaction.

It is a wake up call which says: "Something is wrong. Something is stacked and not flowing. I need to find a way to break through this".

You get jealous because you see others succeeding in areas where you are failing.

Jealousy is your way to keep on fighting and competing.

This will however intensify the feeling of frustration.

The only reason you might want to be mean towards others is because you feel powerless.

The moment you get more satisfaction in your own life and reach your personal targets, frustration and other negative feelings naturally disappear.

When you feel empowered and satisfied about your own existence, you do enjoy celebrating other people's victories as much as yours.

Remember keywords like synergy and win-win when you are in these situations

Focus on finding the exact balance between competing and collaborating.

Let's go back to couple situations.

www.vitalcoaching.com

Are you consumed by jealousy?

Is jealousy destroying your life and your relationship?

It can feel painful, right?

You have visions popping in your mind and it creates pain and insecurity.

Insecurity is a lack of power. Your mind is under attack.

Soft approaches do not work with jealousy.

Of course, you can nurture your feelings, "reason" your emotions and give yourself some time to survive what is happening.

However, when jealousy is consuming your life, it is time to take drastic measures and learn how to deal with this emotional reaction!

Jealousy is destructive when it is suppressed. If you don't take action, you and the relationship will be the victims. Jealousy can be a relationship killer. It can be a self esteem and confidence killer.

If you want to tame jealousy you need one simple thing: Extra power.

Jealousy is the number one relationship challenge.

Extreme jealousy is a powerful response.

Jealousy is here to help.

The reason it becomes extreme is because it does not find a natural channel of expression.

It builds up, saturates and then creates this turbulent flow of emotions.

What do you need to tame your response?

Extra power and determination.

You are on the right track. This is not an illusion. It is a true solution and it works.

www.vitalcoaching.com

Is jealousy consuming you?

It is a battle, right?

This battle happens in your mind and you want to win.

You are not a victim. You are a winner!

www.vitalcoaching.com

Is there another way?

The real alternative to jealousy is complicity.

This is what works best!

However you need two partners on a same wave length to make it work.

Sometimes, you partner is simply not "available".

He might truly be turned on by this woman and be dreaming about it.

If you question him, he'll usually feel attacked and pressured.

So, what to do?

The real reason you feel jealous is because you feel powerless.

You need his love and attention and right now, his mind is somewhere else.

If he can't give it to you, where do you find extra power and validation?

What can stop you from being insecure right now?

What can give you extra trust and confidence?

If your partner does not respond, where can you find these qualities?

What you need is extra power, right?

Your emotional foundation is vulnerable. You feel threatened and call for his protection and validation. He does not respond.

What do you do?

Call upon another force.

I know this is tough, but if you are totally dependent on your partner for inner security, then you are in trouble no matter what.

What you need is extra power.

www.vitalcoaching.com

Where do you find it?

The real issue is personal power. Jealousy is simply an emotional reaction and your best "shot" in such situation.

You do your best and simply use the tools you have. There is nothing wrong with jealousy itself. What is missing is inner power.

It is confidence and emotional security.

Gaining inner power is the real target.

Can you see that? If you had extra power, you would feel totally confident.

You see your partner chatting with another girl. It does not reach you.

On the way home, you tease him: "Hey! Nice chick aye? This girl you were talking with... Looks like a real bitch! Was she expensive? Does she do that for money?"

You see, it is different when you tease.

You can tease only if you have a high level of confidence.

You still express jealousy but in a different way.

Let's call it playful jealousy.

You don't engage in a fierce full battle.

You rather play with these emotions and give your partner some space to fantasize.

At the same time, you stay "out of reach".

Will he go and sleep with her? Probably not.

He is with you.

You might even have the best sex you ever had just after that.

Something very special happens in such an evening.

Your relationship breathes.

www.vitalcoaching.com

You survive a key relationship test.

You grow stronger. You have fun.

This is the same evening that I described earlier n the beginning of this book. These are the same initial events.

What shifts, though is the outcome and the way you stand in it.

www.vitalcoaching.com

When jealousy consumes you

"Obsessive jealousy" is not only destructive for your relationship; it is as well destructive for you as an individual.

Can you feel this irrational response consuming you and your energy?

It is draining.

It is an emotional reaction which destroys your life.

It is not different from negative thinking.

It is simply and emotional loop which keeps turning in circles and goes nowhere.

Can you see that?

When you deal with your own jealousy, you deal with a positive source of power which does not find an effective channel of expression.

The problem is not jealousy.

The problem is lack of skills to use this source of power in an effective way.

Jealousy is a form of power.

www.vitalcoaching.com

Why do you overreact?

The reason you overreact is because of lack of power and insecurity.

Obsessive jealousy results from you inability to effectively protect your relationship.

In fact, your mind is invaded by an emotional reaction you would rather not have, right?

Being obsessively jealous is a sign of weakness.

It is related with a lack of confidence.

What is overreacting? It is your instinctual nature.

Jealousy is an instinctual response.

It is like shivering when you get cold.

You feel another woman's psychic presence and you simply react to it.

Why do you react? Because you feel vulnerable.

Her psychic presence invades your mind and you simply react to it.

Trust and complicity!

Trust and complicity are effective complements to positive jealousy.

When you trust him, you empower him.

You give strength and stimulate him to be faithful.

Infidelities come from a desire to run away. It is a way of escaping your control.

How do you create trust?

- With open communication
- By challenging each other
- By being each other's partner for success

Relationships can sometimes feel constricting.

The goal is to open your life space, not to limit it.

Being in a relationship is not the art of limiting each other; it is the art of partnering for each other's success.

Create synergy.

Create true and meaningful partnership.

This is why trust is the perfect alternative to unwanted jealousy.

Trust is empowering for both of you.

It generates harmony, protection, life force.

How do you build up trust?

By choosing for trust whenever you can.

It is simple: trust is a choice.

It is a message you send to yourself. You tame an obsessive jealousy reaction by feeding yourself with trust.

www.vitalcoaching.com

Communicate! Talk about your relationship's "taboos".

Talk about the limits of your relationship.

What is okay? What is not?

Don't hide yourself in a dream world of pure romantic escape.

Relationships are not only about love; they are about power dynamics as well.

Trust is this solid pillar which sustains your couple.

Can you see how it works?

Trusting is like stepping on a bridge.

In the beginning, you can wonder if it will be solid enough.

This bridge is a relationship between you and your partner.

It takes courage, faith and awareness to step on the bridge and empower this life line you can share with those around you.

www.vitalcoaching.com

Ask yourself

About trust and complicity, ask yourself:

- **Are these qualities present in your relationship?**

- **Do you want more of them?**

- **What do the words trust and complicity mean to you?**

- **What would <u>you</u> do to make them stronger in you and in what you share with your partner?**

What is trust?

When you answer these questions, you expand your awareness about trust and how it works. It gives you clues on where and how to find it in you:

- **What does the word "trust" mean for you?**

- **Describe a few situations in life where you feel immense trust and confidence**

- **If you had to choose between two mind sets: Trust and Insecurity, which one would you choose?**

- **Why is that?**

- **Can you tell me again which one would you choose?**

- **Are there any "risks" involved in trusting?**

- **What exactly happens when you simply trust?**

www.vitalcoaching.com

Part 9 - Your exes and male friends

Why am I jealous if I see my ex with his new girlfriend?

Well, it's very simple!

You used to be together and when you were together you developed a natural desire to protect your relationship.

Jealousy is simply the expression of that desire to protect your couple.

Whenever another woman would come closer to your boyfriend, you would wake up this emotional reaction which sounds like:

"It's with me he is. Stay away from him!"

Yes! This is jealousy!

And there is nothing wrong with expressing small dozes of it as long as you aren't enslaved by it.

Now, what happens when you break up?

You end a relationship but some of the emotional conditioning associated with your ex stays in your mind.

You might feel desire for him, be slightly possessive, or even imagine your future with him even though you rationally know that you are no longer together.

To stop the jealousy pattern, you need to consciously reprogram your mind and develop a new set of emotions when you are around him:

- We are no longer together
- He is free
- He is with another woman
- Our relationship is over
- I don't want to control him
- Etc.

www.vitalcoaching.com

Your ex has a new partner

Your ex is dating a new girl.

You feel jealous.

What do you do?

Of course, this is again a situation where your jealousy response is no longer wanted.

You are both free.

You don't want to claim him anymore.

You really get your full emotional freedom back when you too have someone new in your life.

Why is that?

Because when you break up, emotional attachment to your ex tends to stay in your mind.

You still react to his presence as if he did belong to you.

It stays this way until you create a fresh connection with a new man.

Consciously tell to yourself:

"What he does is none of my business any more."

"We are both free."

Clear your personal space by removing memories of his presence as well.

Check the book "How to get your power back after he breaks up" for more on this. It is available on vitalcoaching.com.

www.vitalcoaching.com

Jealous of your ex partner's new relationship

When you break up with your partner, your ex will probably meet someone else.

This creates jealousy as well.

When you partner with someone, there is always some form of mutual control involved.

Jealousy is an expression of this control.

Control is a sustaining force for the relationship.

It is a power which keeps things together.

The moment you break up, you stop working on the relationship but some emotional patterns tend to survive the break up.

The moment you see your ex with someone else, you have a "claiming" reaction: "Hey! That's <u>my</u> man!"

You know it is not the truth but you still did not train your emotions to react differently.

<u>It is a left over conditioning</u>.

Being a bit jealous is okay as long as it does not consume you.

If it consumes you, it means that you are still too invested in your ex.

What is the way to solve this reaction? <u>Let go!</u>

Consciously train your response:

"Hey, I am really happy for you. It is good that you and I can move on and stay friends. Can I introduce you to my new boyfriend?"

You might fake it in the beginning. But with some repetition, this will become your new mind set.

www.vitalcoaching.com

The moment you let go of something you can't control, it is immensely liberating.

My ex is chatting it up with other girls on Facebook!

The key word here is "Ex".

This tells you straight away that jealousy is unjustified.

It does appear, sure!

But it's an emotion which is totally useless in this situation.

In other words, you don't want it!

It drains your energy!

You want to get rid of it! You want to go to battle so that the jealousy response disappears forever out of your mind.

Guess what? It is within your range to achieve just that!

What about feeling really angry towards him?

Well, anger is a different story!

Why? Because anger is actually here to serve you.

Let's dive into it...

Anger is a fire or power trying to break free in you.

Anger is actually the reflection of a freeing force breaking through your body and mind.

Imagine a volcano ready to explode because the lava or inner power is being constricted.

When you break up you need to free yourself from your ex.

Anger is the awakening of this inner freeing fire.

Anger is okay! It is actually good and natural and trying to suppress it will be counterproductive.

Now, you are not allowed to act on it or hurt anyone with this anger.

www.vitalcoaching.com

You need to find other ways of channeling it until your system "digests" it.

The best is to go to the gym and do some power training. You can do that outdoor as well. You can focus on your career or launch a new business.

All these are creative expressions of your fire-anger.

Remember!!!! You are not allowed to hurt yourself or anyone else!

No vindictive action!

See anger as a creative fire which can open new doors in your life.

It destroys the past and creates new space for your new future to be born.

Without this inner fire you would stay stacked in old patterns you no longer want.

www.vitalcoaching.com

Can you be jealous of a secret crush?

Imagine that you are secretly attracted to a guy at work.

You might be building a flirty connection without dating.

One day, you see him chatting with another girl and see yourself getting jealous about it.

Okay!

This is typically a situation in which jealousy is unjustified and has the power to mess up everything!!!!

If he feels an inch of your jealousy it will definitely destroy the light connection you have with him.

Flirting with someone does not give you the right to claim that person.

There is no commitment and no relationship yet.

You are both free!

Flirting is just flirting!

It is light, fun and non-committed.

Claiming him because he flirts with you is the biggest mistake you can make in such situation!

Expressing possessiveness in that situation is a fun killer for everyone involved!

www.vitalcoaching.com

Jealous when your friend with benefits finds another woman?

Friend with benefits means that you are intimate but not committed, right?

That's the deal.

This means that you both agreed that dating other people was okay.

Of course, being in this type of open relationship or love triangle is extra challenging.

Most people don't want to take it.

This is why they choose a committed relationship instead.

If you want to keep your intimate connection with that friend, here are a couple of ideas.

Any time you feel jealousy, reason yourself and go back to ideas like:

- He is free
- He does what he wants
- I have no right to tell him what to do!
- This is what we agreed in the first place

You create a new mind set and emotional reactions for the exact challenge you face.

This means reconditioning (don't be scared! It's a good thing) yourself to respond differently.

www.vitalcoaching.com

Male friend spends all his time with his new partner!

It's already tough to deal with jealousy issues when you are in a committed relationship!

Now, when you are friends, even best friends with someone, there is no commitment!

How can you claim someone who does not belong to you?!!!

In that situation, jealousy is an absolute waste of your time and energy!

It is destructive and frustrating for all those involved.

Get rid of that pattern and learn to be happy for him.

Conclusion

I hope you enjoyed this material!

Feed back? Questions? Success stories?

Email me at francisco@vitalcoaching.com

For coaching:

http://vitalcoaching.com/coaching.htm

For more topics on dating and personal power go to:

http://vitalcoaching.com

To your power!

Francisco Bujan

Made in the USA
Lexington, KY
03 May 2012